Recreating Eden

From John Parkinson's *Paradisi in Sole*, 1629

Recreating Eden

A NATURAL HISTORY OF
BOTANICAL GARDENS

Mary Soderstrom

Véhicule Press

Véhicule Press acknowledges the on-going support of the Canada Council for the arts and the aid of the Book Publishers Industry Program of the Department of Canadian Heritage.

Cover design by J.W. Stewart
Front cover image: The Clusius Garden, Hortus Botanicus, Leiden
Cover imaging: André Jacob
All colour photographs, including colour plates and cover
are by Mary Soderstrom.
Special assistance: Vicki Marcok and H. Bruce Henry
Set in Minion by Simon Garamond
Printing: AGMV-Marquis Inc.

CATALOGUING IN PUBLICATION DATA

Soderstrom, Mary, 1942-
Recreating Eden : a natural history of botanical gardens

ISBN 1-55065-151-X

1. Botanical gardens-Guidebooks. I. Title.

QK71.S62 2001   712'.5   C2001-900276-9

Véhicule Press
www.vehiculepress.com

Distributed in the United States by LPC Group
800-243-0138
Distributed in Canada by General Distribution Services
800-387-0141 (Ontario & Quebec); 800-387-0172

Printed in Canada on alkaline paper.

"The world goes round"

– Lee Soderstrom

Contents

III

Gardens of the Twentieth Century

A Garden to Educate and Delight

The Flowers of San Francisco

A University Garden on the Western Shore

~✿~

~✿~

Acknowledgements

MANY THANKS to my sister Laurie and her husband Mik Down, who listened to me talk about the project more than necessary and who provided hospitality again and again; Adrienne and John Hickman, good friends who put me up not once but twice when I visited Strybing in San Francisco; John and Barbara Yellowlees, who gave me the Martha Stewart room when I visited the UBC gardens; Ted and Betty Lou Bradshaw, who shared their love for the UC Berkeley Botanical Garden with me as well as provided much hospitality; Helen Lim and Alain Polguère, who opened many doors in Singapore for me; Mollie and Dick Down who shared their garden and much more with me in London; my husband Lee who may have visited more gardens than he cared to; our daughter Elin who showed us Holland; and our son Lukas who watched my back in Manhattan and generally held down the fort.

In the gardens themselves (in order of the age of the garden): Prefect Jan de Koning, Gerda Uffellen and Constance van der Veen of the Hortus Botanicus at the University of Leiden; Yves-Marie Allain, director of the Service des cultures of the Jardin des Plantes in Paris; Peter Crane, director of the Royal Botanic Gardens, Kew; Chin See Chung, director of the Singapore Botanic Gardens: Peter Raven, director of the Missouri Botanical Garden; Karl Lauby, vice-president for communications at the New York Botanical Garden; Jean-Jacques Lincourt, director of the Jardin botanique de Montréal, and former director Pierre Bourque, now mayor of Montreal; Scot Medbury, director of Strybing Arboretum and Botanical Garden, and Bian Tan, manager of plant collections there; David Tarrant and Douglas Justice of the University of British Columbia Botanical Garden; Moura Quayle, dean of UBC's School of Agriculture; Roy Taylor, former director of the UBC Botanical Garden.

Also thanks to the Bellingham Public Library, Washington, which had both John Prest's *The Garden of Eden: The Botanic Garden and the*

Re-Creation of Paradise and *Great Botanical Gardens of the World* by Edward Hyams, with photographs by William Macquitty, the books that got me started. The staff at the libraries and archives of the Jardin botanique de Montréal, the Canadian Centre for Architecture, the University of British Columbia, and the Westmount Public Library were also extremely helpful.

In the Beginning...

IN THE BEGINNING was the garden.

In the Mosaic tradition it is called the Garden of Eden; in other cultures it has different names. It is a place of abundance, peace, and joy, from which humans wandered or were expelled, and for which men and women have yearned ever since.

It is even the place where religious belief and modern ideas about evolution meet, for evolutionary scientists agree with scripture: humankind's beginning was in a sort of garden. We evolved in a landscape where, during seasons of good rains, people had food aplenty: flowering trees dotted green grasslands, streams flowed down from hills, and animals were sleek and abundant. Scientists contend it was on the fertile plains of East Africa that humans evolved over hundreds of thousands of years. We are descended from those who were good at reading that landscape for its clues about food, water, and safety. Remnants of that ability show up in many ways, from the sacred stories we tell to the kind of parks we enjoy.

This is a book about the attempts of people to recapture green and well-watered landscapes—to remake Eden—and where that quest has led us. The journey has lasted several hundred years. Individuals have done the searching, but usually they have done so with the idea that their actions bettered humankind, one way or another. Such altruism may seem naive at the dawn of a new century where few speak about a collective good. Most would say that all they really want to do is cultivate their own gardens. In the long run, we are all in this together, however. This green planet is the only one we have.

This book is also about scientific thinking. Humans are animals, after all, and all animals have mechanisms for choosing where to graze or to hunt, to rest, or to bear their young. Ornithologists think that it is the arrangement of branches which say to many birds that food and shelter will be good here. The reaction is immediate; the calculation is automatic.

Humans have developed cultures, but we *also* have automatic responses to nature. Research indicates that people in different societies prefer the same shapes of trees. Most of us like open, grassy landscapes, shun dry terrain and trees that look diseased, and feel more peaceful by the side of a stream or lake. What signaled good hunting and gathering on the savanna still pleases us today.

Gardens play an important role in many of our mythologies. The Greeks described Arcadia and the Garden of Hesperides where the daughters of Atlas guarded the golden apples of Hera. Muslims envision the walled gardens of Paradise which await the faithful. And then there is Eden, where the Mosaic tradition says we began. "And God said," the King James Version of the Bible has it, "behold I have given you every herb bearing seed which is upon the face of all the earth, and every tree, in which is there fruit of a tree yielding seed: to you it shall be for meat."

But Adam and Eve went and ate from the Tree of Knowledge, and were barred from Eden for all time. After that it was work by the sweat of our brows, and thorns, and thistles, and difficult childbirth. The Bible story is, in fact, an apt metaphor for what scientists think happened as we evolved. The selective pressure was for bigger brains and more intelligence, which first allowed movement into every niche where men and women could hunt and gather, and, later brought about the development of farming. Agriculture is hard work, although it eventually supported more people than hunting and gathering. But having those big-brained, intelligent babies is painful and hazardous for both mother and child. It is not surprising that our traditions refer to an idyllic past time.

Today, however, it is hard for many of us to imagine that the history of the world as recounted in the first five books of the Bible was taken as the literal truth by most followers of the Mosaic tradition until the middle of the last century. That meant that nearly everyone in the Western world believed that Eden once existed. Many reasoned that Eden might have survived Noah's Flood and could still be hidden someplace.

Prester John was a legendary Christian in either India or Africa, and Eden

Apple tree.
J. Foord. *Decorative Plant and Flower Studies*, 1906.

was said to lie on the other side of his kingdom. Members of the Portuguese royal family were convinced of Prester John's existence, and part of the Portuguese expeditionary surge in the fifteenth century was fired by the desire to find his kingdom.

The Bible says that Eden lay at the headwaters of a river which branched to form four great rivers, the Euphrates, the Hiddekel, the Physion, and the Gihon. Since the first of these is in Arabia, the search for Eden was initially centered there, but because no burning torch was found guarding Eden's gate, other rivers were suggested as possibilities. When the Portuguese passed the mouths of the Senegal, the Gambia, the Niger, and the Zaire as they worked their way down the coast of Africa, they thought it possible that Eden might lie in the heart of that continent, perhaps in the highlands of Ethiopia.

A copy of the second-century Greek geographer Ptolemy's work reached Florence in 1400 where it was quickly translated into Latin. This opened new possibilities. If Eden lay in the east as many Christian authorities believed, Ptolemy's maps suggested that it might be reached by sailing west around the world. Indeed Christopher Columbus (1451-1506) included in his crew a converted Jew who knew Hebrew and Arabic because he believed the man would be useful as an interpreter if the expedition happened upon Eden.

What Columbus and others found in both the New World and the areas of Africa and Asia previously unknown to Europeans was enough to undermine religious tradition. Those hitherto undreamed-of plants and animals in the Americas raised questions. Were they created at the same time as all the flora and fauna familiar to Europeans? Or were there perhaps two creations? Had parts of the world escaped the flood? The European discoveries offered a challenge that had not been available to humans since Eden, that of naming and describing the unfamiliar plants and animals.

With that challenge came another: could it be possible to bring the old and new together in a present-day Eden? Why not try, proposed the founders of the first botanic gardens in the sixteenth century. They suggested that "since each plant was a created thing, and God had revealed a part of himself in each thing that he created, a complete collection of all the things created by God must reveal God completely."

A collection of all things created by God? Europeans brought home samples of what they found as they explored the world which was unknown to them. They named plants. They propagated them. They learned to control them. The gardens became both living museums designed to delight and elegant laboratories for experiments in botany.

What follows in this book is an exploration of how these gardens have evolved over the last 400 years. Like the plants they fostered, the first gardens sent out shoots that have flourished in a wide variety of climates. And, also like the plants, they have evolved to exploit the advantages of their particular surroundings. What remains a constant, however, is how we react to them. What remains a question is what we are going to do to protect them and the green world from which they spring.

I spent my childhood in Southern California where plants grow year round, given enough water. My parents gardened in fits and starts: Bermuda grass and pickle weed as ground cover; blue plumbago which grew to cover the front of the house; a few rather sad roses; bougainvillea that climbed a patio wall; geraniums three feet high that nevertheless required little care. These were all part of the background to which I paid little mind, unless called upon to mow the lawn or to water the garden. I did not know that all these plants, along with the eucalyptus which marched down the alley behind the house, were transplants from somewhere else, the result of botanizing by someone in the eighteenth or nineteenth century in Chile or Africa, Brazil, or China.

In the series of apartments I lived in as a young adult in Northern California I rooted ivy cuttings and sweet potatoes to provide some cheap greenery. It was not until I moved to Montreal that I developed a thirst for plants. Here, where the vegetable world shuts down for six months of the year, I started growing house plants more or less seriously. I also discovered that a visit to the greenhouses of the Jardin botanique de Montréal was a quick antidote to cabin fever in the middle of winter.

The Montreal garden has become one of my favorite places, whether in winter when the snow drifts up on the windows of the glass houses, or in spring when the lilacs are in bloom, or in summer. Well, you get the picture. I have spent many pleasant hours there, often with kids in tow.

Sea fig, or pickle weed as the author remembers it being called, where she grew up in Southern California.
Drawing by Margaret Armstrong, 1915.

And more than once, as my own tiny city garden developed, I have used the garden's horticultural service to help solve a problem.

A book about botanical gardens never occurred to me until I began to do research for a biography of Robert Nelson, a Montreal physician and politician. Because he spent some time in London during the 1820s studying medicine and anatomy, I did quite a bit of reading about the state of science in the first part of the nineteenth century. There is no direct link between medicine and The Royal Botanical Gardens at Kew but as I read, it became clear that exciting things were happening in the biological sciences in England at that time. From there it was not too far a hop to Kew, botanical gardens in general, and eventually this book.

But what is a botanical garden? Whenever I told people that I was writing a book about them, I was flooded with suggestions. Had I seen the Jardin de Métis on the Lower Saint Lawrence? What about the Rose Garden in Berkeley? The Butchard Garden on Vancouver Island? The Chelsea Physick Garden in London? Versailles?

In each case I had to reply that I would love to see them (and over the years I spent researching this book I was able to see many), but, I would stress, I was not writing about gardens, but a particular kind of garden, a botanical garden. That sounds like a tautology—any garden is, strictly speaking, botanical, ("of or pertaining to plants" says *Webster's Collegiate Dictionary*). I was interested in those botanical gardens in which plants from all over the world were brought together in a systematic fashion to be studied. The reasons given for this gathering-in has varied over time, as we shall see, but there are three constants. Botanical gardens have always been thought of as useful places; the gardens' *raisons d'être* have been described in philosophical terms, and people have taken delight in them.

Humans have collected plants ever since someone realized that planting seeds meant that new plants would appear in the next growing season. Archeologists date the beginning of agriculture to about 12,000 years ago, a mere yesterday in the long history of humankind's development. The next step, gardens for pleasure and study, certainly existed in ancient times. Nekht, head gardener at the Temple Garden at Karnak, is supposed to have drawn up the first garden plan under the rule of Pharaoh Thotmes III more than 3,000 years ago. About the same time, on the other side of the world, the Chinese emperor Shen Nung had a garden where he collected plants from China and from far away to test their medicinal uses. Among them was the gingko, that living fossil, which is the only surviving species from a genus gone extinct millions of years ago. In the seventh century B.C., King Sennacherib's garden at Nineveh was said to have rare plants, while a hundred years later, Nebuchadnezzar II built the terrace gardens in Babylon which came to be known as the Hanging Gardens, one of the seven wonders of the ancient world.

The Greek Xenophon (c. 430-355 B.C) first used the word *parádeisos* which has become linked in our minds with Eden, when talking about the gardens of the Persian kings and nobles. The word itself is formed from two old Iranian words—*pairi*, around, and *daêza*, wall. The image of a walled garden, green and secluded in a hot climate, springs immediately to mind.

Greek philosopher and scientist Aristotle (385-322 B.C.) also had a garden, and his pupil, Alexander the Great (356-323 B.C), is supposed to have sent plants from the countries he conquered in his victorious march eastward. Aristotle's colleague and successor Theophrastus (372-287 B.C.) became the botanist-curator of the garden. Some give him credit with developing the first garden where plants were studied in a systematic way, but it was not until the Renaissance that botanical gardens as we understand them today were planted. The first date from the 1540s in Italy, at Pisa and Padua. Today there are hundreds of them all over the world.

So why focus on the nine gardens in this book?

The first, the Hortus Botanicus in Leiden, the Netherlands, was actually the last I visited, and then only because I was in the neighborhood. When I saw it, I was ashamed. Not only was the garden quite lovely, but its history obviously was deep and important. Started in 1590, it is usually considered the third oldest botanical garden and it was the garden of the extensive Dutch empire. Yet because it was not part of the English- or French-speaking world, I knew practically nothing about it even though by the time I visited I had read extensively about botanical gardens and visited many. The experience was a valuable reminder that one must not forget that what one sees depends upon where one sits, and when dealing with big questions like humankind's relation to nature, the widest possible vision is required.

The next two gardens, the Jardin des Plantes in Paris and the Royal Gardens at Kew are obvious choices. They are the gardens of the French and English empires, respectively. The next three are gardens modeled on the Imperial gardens, particularly Kew: the Singapore Botanic Gardens, the Missouri Botanical Garden at St. Louis, and the New York Botanical Garden. The final three gardens are gardens of the twentieth century, which owe their existence in part to ideas about how society should be organized which were current at the time: the Jardin botanique de Montréal, the Strybing Arboretum and Botanical Garden in San Francisco, and the University of British Columbia Botanical Garden at Vancouver.

Recreating Eden is intended to be more than a guidebook to gardens. The reasons why people make gardens lie at the very heart of human nature. The effort to understand and to appreciate gardens properly has summoned up elegant theories and employed some great minds. But gardeners are a practical lot, usually. They literally have their feet on the ground. So, while we explore the intellectual and theological side of gardening, we will stroll through some of the world's best and most interesting gardens.

Gardens of Empire

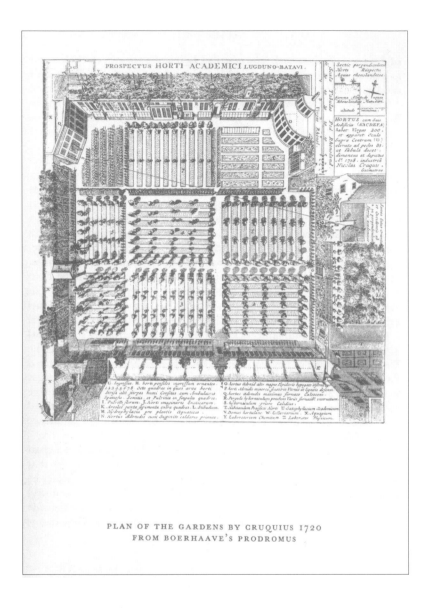

PLAN OF THE GARDENS BY CRUQUIUS 1720
FROM BOERHAAVE'S PRODROMUS

One of the several plans of the Hortus Botanicus.

The Garden of the Dutch Empire

THE HORTUS BOTANICUS, the botanical garden at the University of Leiden, owes its existence to burghers who chose a university rather than a tax cut.

In the sixteenth century what is now known as Holland was under control of the Spanish. The Spanish king Phillip II (1527-1598) claimed part of France and most of the Western Hemisphere in addition to Portugal and the Low Countries. For eighty years, from 1568 to 1648, the Dutch struggled against foreign domination, and twice Leiden was besieged. As a reward for the stalwart way the Leiden citizens held out against the Spanish threat, William the Silent (1533-1584, the founder of the House of Orange which reigns in Holland today) offered the city either four years' exemption from taxes or a university.

Long-sighted and canny Leiden opted for the university, which opened in 1575. It became one of the premier centers of learning in Europe; the great international lawyer Hugo Grotius taught there in the years following its establishment, as did the French philosopher René Descartes. In 1590 the Hortus Botanicus was founded. Within a few years it became a great botanical garden under the leadership of one of the first botanists, Charles de l'Escluse (1526-1609), also known by his Latin name Clusius.

Today you can see the garden as he planned it by taking a fifteen minute walk from the Leiden railway station along canals and past a few recent buildings and many handsome houses which date from the seventeenth century. Turn right at Rapenburg 73, pass a dark brick university administration building, and go into a courtyard. There you will find yourself at the entrance to the botanical garden. A new palm house faces older laboratory buildings across a garden filled with seasonal flowers. To see where things began, cross the small canal and turn left at the junction of paths. The entrance to the Clusius Garden is halfway down the length of the garden. Cross a little bridge, open the big gate in the high wall and you will find yourself transported back to 1594.

At first glance you may think you are in the "physick" or medicinal plant garden of a medieval cloister or medical school. The pattern is a square, more or less, divided into four quadrants which are themselves further sub-divided. Espaliered trees grow along the walls. Over to the side in a small extension are fruit trees and six old fashioned beehives. Bees bustle in and out. "God feeds all Creatures" is carved on a plaque in Dutch on the wall.

But this is much more than a garden of plants whose medicinal virtues had been described by Dioscorides, the second-century pharmacist-doctor whose five volumes of herbal lore were standard texts throughout Europe by the late Renaissance. Nor are the plants growing here only those which have a place in the traditions of local folk healing. This garden has plants from many different places, arranged so that they can be compared and studied easily. Like the first botanic gardens founded at Padua and Pisa fifty years before, the Hortus Botanicus was established with the twin objects of glorifying God's creation and studying what wonders he had wrought in the plant world.

Italy was the cradle of the Renaissance so it is not surprising that the first modern botanical gardens were developed there. But why did Leiden's Hortus Botanicus, a 2.6 hectare (6.4 acre) garden in a provincial town develop into something so special?

Unlike the French and British, the Dutch never called their colonial holdings an empire, and today the Dutch language is mother tongue to only twenty million people in the Netherlands and former colonies. That is a paltry number compared to the 332 million people outside of Spain who claim Spanish as their mother tongue. To suppose that the Dutch never amounted to much on the world scene, however, is to misunderstand seriously the role the Dutch played in European exploration.

The Hortus Botanicus was planted a hundred years after Columbus' first voyage of discovery. Europeans had not only sailed west to the Americas, they had also rounded Africa and begun to trade across the Indian Ocean by sailing east to India and the Spice Islands of Southeast Asia. The Spanish, Portuguese, and British were in the forefront of this exploration, but by the end of the sixteenth century the Dutch were taking their place as adventurous traders and explorers.

Carolus Clusius.
Engraving by de Geijn.
Courtesy of Hortus Botanicus.

The defeat of the Spanish Armada, sent in 1588 by the Catholic King Philip II to remove Protestant Elizabeth I (1533-1603) from the English throne, was a cruel blow to Spanish sea power. After the Spanish defeat overseas expeditions by the Dutch and the English increased mightily. Both set up East Indies trading companies early in the 1600s. Their attempts to colonize North America began within a few years of each other; the first (but unsuccessful) English attempt was in Virginia in 1607 while the Dutch started their colony at what is now New York in 1612.

THE DUTCH GOLDEN AGE
This was the beginning of Dutch Golden Age, which saw a flowering of the arts and sciences. Rembrandt, Vermeer, and Hals painted their masterworks then, Van Leeunhoeck invented microbiology with his microscope, and

Spinoza and Descartes developed their philosophies. Part of this cultural ferment was fueled by riches arriving regularly from the Spice Islands and Southeast Asia in the small, fast Dutch ships. Investors earned a 30 percent return on their money during the first ten years after the Dutch East India Company began operation in 1609.

Seeds, plants, and other curiosities came back to Europe with every successful voyage. In addition, missions to the Ottoman Empire had been sending botanical treasures like the tulip from the Near East and beyond for decades.

The University of Leiden's trustees (called the Curatores) succeeded without much trouble in getting the city to set aside a plot of land for a garden and for a house for the professor of medicine who would be in charge of it. Finding the proper person to design the garden, however, was more difficult. Clusius would have been an ideal choice from the beginning because he was not only a brilliant botanist who had planned several gardens, but also he was fluent in Dutch (his first translation was of a botanical work from that language into French.) But the Curatores first asked a professor of medicine from Padua, who turned them down because his wife did not like Leiden. Then the Curatores asked Clusius, who also turned them down straight away. The refusal was probably not surprising, since Clusius was in his sixties and in poor health. For several years he had been established in Frankfurt, busily translating botanical texts from one of the seven languages in which he was fluent into another. A native of Artois in the part of Flanders now in France, he had spent his life collecting and describing plants all over Europe after studies in first in law and then medicine. In his thirties he had spent two years travelling in Spain and Portugal, where he collected more than 200 species, and came across Garcia da Orta's Portuguese work on the plants of India, which he translated into Latin. Later he also translated a Spanish book on the plants of the New World into Latin, a book on medicinal plants of the Portuguese Indies, as well as Sir Walter Raleigh's account of his expedition to Virginia.

Translation was only part of his work. He had written treatises on the flora of Spain, Austria, and Hungary, corresponded with every botanist of note in Europe, and collected and distributed plants and bulbs. His fellow botanists at the botanical garden at Pisa thought so highly of him that they put his portrait on display in the university's entry hall, the only foreigner among a bevy of great Italian naturalists. He also wrote the first monographs

Hyacinthus stellatus.
Clusius. *Rariorum plantarum historia*, 1601.

Delphiniusm elatius.
Clusius. *Rariorum plantarum historia*, 1601.

on the tulip and the rhododendron, as well as designing gardens for the Emperor Maxmilian II of Austria and many members of the nobility.

Behind all his work lay a belief that the beauty of plants was a reflection of the wonders of God's creation and the harmony of the universe.

THE CLUSIUS GARDEN

The university's trustees pressed Clusius to accept. He would not have to give lectures, they assured him, "only in summer when the herbs are strong and fresh he might go daily to the Gardens in the afternoon to answer those that ask for the names, the history and the virtues of these plants." To that he was agreeable, so long as he could have a servant to help him. "It be far from me that I would deprive the youth from anything from which I have gained knowledge by long experience," he wrote in the summer of 1592. The Curatores named an apothecary from Delft, Dirck Outgaerszoon Cluyt, to be his assistant. An inspired appointment. As Clusius and Clutius, they oversaw the birth of a garden which soon had more than 1,000 different sorts of plants, and together they wrote a treatise on beekeeping.

Clusius had access to plants from every corner of the world through his network of correspondents and colleagues. From the moment he agreed to come to Leiden, he started sending seeds, bulbs, and tubers there in preparation for planting the garden. One list prepared in 1592 shows more than 250 specimens sent that first summer, although from a list made in 1594, it looks as if not many germinated or survived the winter.

It is thanks to these early lists and scale drawings that in the 1930s the Hortus Botanicus's prefect H. Veendorp and and garden director, L.G.M. Baas Becking, were able to reconstruct the first garden. It was a labour of love which they recount in a history of the garden published for its 350th anniversary.

Rather early in the University's history, other buildings had been constructed around the original Clusius garden, and additional botanical collections were planted on land to the west. An enormous copper beech tree shaded much of the original garden when Veendorp and Baas Becking set about recreating it. However, the university came up with another piece of ground not far away. Lying between the former theological college and government building, the parcel of land "seemed a sufficiently characteristic environment to be haunted by the spirits of both Clusius and Clutius," they wrote.

They set to work searching through archives and discovered that many of the plants listed were still growing in the garden, although not in the same places. From their numerous contacts they even received plants thought to have been lost, including a tomato with yellow fruit and a lily of the valley with pink flowers.

They also found a "living link between the present and the early youth of our university" growing where the original Clusius garden had been, a gold chain tree (*laburnum*) which was planted in 1601. It was still flowering in the spring of 2000 near the main entrance to the Hortus Botanicus.

Among the other plants which grew in the garden during its first years were lilacs originally from Southeast Europe, an oriental plane tree planted from seed brought from Crete in 1592, a pistachio from Asia Minor, and what became known as the common horse chestnut, which is also from the Middle East.

The garden had several roses and many varieties of fruit: red, white, and black currants, green and red gooseberries, black mulberries, wine grapes, figs, cherries, and several sorts of plums. Clusius tried to grow melons, too, but they didn't do very well. The yellow tomatoes along with some striped ones appear to have been grown as an ornamentals; the "bad smell of this weed clearly shows how unsuitable it is as a food," says a contemporary Dutch text.

Sea kale, garden cress, endive, asparagus, lettuce, broad beans, pickling cucumbers, lavender, rosemary, dill, sage, common thyme, anise, parsley and celery were also grown.

So were many flowers: single and double-flowered sweet Williams, peonies, cowslips, auriculas, carnations propagated by cuttings "because seedlings usually carried smaller flowers," garden pinks from the Holy Land, Turkey, and Crete, stocks, hollyhocks, poppies, as well as many native flowers, a number of orchids, ferns, may lily, gentians, and yarrow.

The garden had tulips, which Clusius imported from Turkey where the flower is a native. He is credited with being one of the first to promote the tulip in Europe, setting the stage for the tulip mania which was to sweep Holland a few years after his death during the height of the Dutch Golden Age. But Clusius also loved the various lilies, anemones, narcissi, and irises which he imported and planted.

Plants from the Western Hemisphere included the prickly pear (apparently introduced from Sicily where hedges of this New World transplant already grew), American aloe, probably red and yellow peppers, two sorts of tobacco, the nasturtium, and the potato.

Tropical plants like ginger, the castor bean, and sugar cane were grown, although keeping them alive over the winter must have been a chore since heated glass houses were not built until years later.

That the Clusius garden today contains the thousand or so plants it did some 400 years ago is a tribute to the careful records kept by Clusius and his associates and to those who resurrected them to make the garden live again.

In 1938 Veendorp and Baas Becking wrote with understandable pride:

> The old garden in its reconstruction, of course, shows a crowded and rather haphazard aspect to the casual observer. After a few minutes, however, the charm begins to work and in this environment three centuries seem to drop from us. It is a good place to meditate upon the significance of human endeavour and of botany in particular.

That is true still. Refurbished in the 1990s, the Cluisius garden is a wonderful place, but much has happened in the world and in the Hortus Botanicus since its founding.

Linnaeus Names Plants

The systematic garden is an example. Located just off the path to the Clusius Garden, at first glance it looks as if it could be appreciated relatively quickly as one strolls past. But its many beds group plants together according to the botanical family to which they belong. By comparing the leaves, flowers, stems, and other parts, naturalists—professional and amateur—have been able to figure out the relationship between plants. Doing this is called taxonomy and is the foundation of much biological science.

Right in the middle of the beds is a bust of Carl von Linné (1707-1778) the celebrated Swedish botanist who is the father of taxonomy. Like Charles de l'Escluse, he also gave himself a Latin name, Carolus Linnaeus, which is how most of the world remembers him.

When Linnaeus, aged twenty-eight, arrived at Leiden in the early summer of 1735 he had just been granted two academic degrees from another Dutch university, Harderwijk. He had studied medicine at the

Carl von Linné, who adopted the Latin name Linnaeus,
was the founder of modern systematic botany.
He devised a classification system for flowering plants.

University of Uppsala, but found the botanical part of the curriculum far more interesting than medicine. He had organized a botanizing expedition to Lapland in northern Sweden, and another in central Sweden. He'd been thinking deeply about the relationships among plants for some time and was ready to share his ideas with other botanists.

One of those most open to listening was Jan Fredrik Gronovius, a botanist and curator of the University of Leiden. Within a month of his arrival, Linnaeus showed the older man a seven-page manuscript in which he outlined his plan for categorizing the plant and animal world. Gronovius was so impressed that he and a colleague paid for immediate publication. The paper, called *Systema Naturae*, was an outline of what Linnaeus would do during the rest of his career. It was work which would revolutionize the biological sciences by solving the problems of how to tell one species from another, and what to call each species. Two years later he published *Genera Plantarum*, which he dedicated to Herman Boerhaave, a grand old man of botany at the Hortus Botanicus at the time. (Boerhaave, in addition to his own work, was renowned for his support for other botanists. He financed the posthumous publication of a treatise on French flora by a French botanist who had died owing the printer money for plates of the plants featured in the book. He also had 508 drawings by the French priest-botanist Charles Plumier copied after his death so that they could be published.)

While Linnaeus was at Leiden, the garden underwent one of its first major expansions, more than doubling in size. Even though he apparently was eager to return to Sweden, Linnaeus tarried long enough to help the Prefect, Adraan von Royer, reorganize the entire plant collection along lines more in keeping with taxonomic ideas.

One of Linnaeus's major concerns was how to classify all the new glories of the plant world which were being brought back by explorers and botanists. Some way had to be found to standardize names. Although botanists and naturalists used Latin as a common language, there was no clear way to determine which plant was which. For example (as Daniel Boorstin notes in *The Discoverers*), before Clusius went to Leiden he named one species of the morning-glory genus, *Convolvulus folio Althaeae*. Fifty years later the Swiss botanist Gaspard Bauhin (1560-1624) called the same species *Convolvulus argenteus Altheae folio*. Linnaeus first changed this to *Convolvulus foliis ovatis divisis basi truncat: laciniis intermediis duplo longioribus*, and then further elaborated it to *Convolvulus foliss palmatis coradits sericeis: lobis repanids, pendunulis bifloris.*

While this method gave those who knew Latin a good idea of what a plant looked like, it was far too cumbersome, and it did not settle the question of what differentiated one species from another. Aristotle approached the problem by grouping organisms according to criteria which seemed more or less self-evident, and then subdividing each group further. John Ray (1627?-1705), an English botanist, had proposed that species be defined as a group of individual organisms whose offspring resembled themselves.

Clearly Ray's idea could apply to animals, but did it apply to plants in the same way? Plants reproduced, no question about that, but did they have sex? By the beginning of the 1700s, several botanists had begun to believe that they did. Linnaeus was among them. Furthermore, he was convinced that in plant sexuality lay a powerful tool for categorizing plants. Like Clusius, he believed that in studying nature one was also studying the divine order of God's creation. That meant that in constructing a "natural classification" of plants and animals, naturalists would also be revealing God's order in the universe. This lofty aim, combined perhaps with an young man's penchant for poetry, led him to set down his ideas in the most elaborate of terms. In 1729, when he was just twenty-two, he described the sexual part of the flower in terms that might make a modern person think of Georgia O'Keeffe's erotic paintings of flowers:

> The flowers' leaves ... serve as bridal beds which the Creator has so gloriously arranged, adorned with such noble bed curtains, and perfumed with so many soft scents that the bridegroom with his bride might there celebrate their nuptials with so much the greater solemnity. . .

He set up twenty-three classes of flowering plants, based on the "male" organs, the number and length of the stamens. He added a twenty-fourth class, which he called Cryptogamia, which included plants without apparent flowers. He divided the classes of flowering plants into orders on the basis of their female organs, their stigmas and styles. He described each class in terms that some of his contemporaries called "salacious" and "loathsome harlotry." For example, the class Polyandria (from the Greek words meaning many *poly* and male *andros*), which includes the poppy and the linden tree, he described as "twenty males or more in the same bed with the female." (Perhaps it should be noted that Baas Becking and Veendorp mention that during the period Linnaeus was developing these ideas, he turned down a two-year plant collecting trip to the Cape Colony in South Africa on behalf of the Hortus Botanicus. The reason he gave was that he couldn't stand hot climates, but really, according to Baas Becking and Veendorp, he was eager to return to Sweden where his fiancée was waiting for him.)

Linnaeus's system of classification was simple enough, but it did not solve the problem of naming plants. The temptation was always there to qualify the name with a description, although Linnaeus suggested that in the field botanists use the genus name (for example, in the case of the morning glory, *Convolvulus*) and add a reference to the place the plant would be found in one of his lists of plants. Over time he saw that simply adding one short descriptive term to the genus name would serve the same purpose, provided that everyone was aware of the new two-part or binomial name and agreed on it. To this end he undertook the massive job of finding names for the nearly 6,000 species then recognized—and he did it in less than a year.

Linnaeus used a number of strategies to find names: Latin words that described something about the plant's habit of growth (the morning glory's twisting tendrils prompted *convolvulus*, for example), the terrain where it grew, or the Latin form of the plant's common name. And a large number

Morning Glory (*Convolvulus*).
Emanuel Sweerts. *Florilegium*, 1612.

of plants new to Europe received Latinized forms of the name of their first collector or propagator. One of them is the black locust (*Robinia pseudo-acacia*), an American tree native to a relatively restricted area of the Carolina and Virginia mountains. It was introduced to Europe about 1635, and grown by Jean Robin, the gardener at the precursor to the Jardin des Plantes in Paris. Linnaeus named it after him, but a specimen of the tree had arrived at the Hortus Botanicus nearly 100 years earlier: it is listed in the 1641 catalogue.

Today binomial names are standard throughout biology, but the ways of classifying and establishing relationships among species have shifted to take into account more than just the form of the plants' sexual parts. The bust of Linnaeus at Leiden now surveys a systemic garden laid out according to the taxonomic ideas of the American botanist Ledyard Stebbins which considers the genetic structure of plants and other physical features.

Plants from Warm Climates

In mid-summer the section of the garden directly across from the systemic garden is a showcase for plants from tropical and Mediterranean climates. They can be grown outside only during the long days of summer sunlight, even though many of them have been cultivated in plant houses at Leiden since the first voyages of the Dutch East India Company. At the beginning the Hortus seems to have played a rather small role in transferring plants from one part of the world for commercial ends. Notes from the early period mention several unsuccessful attempts to grow cinnamon trees, which were found by the Dutch when they took control of Ceylon. And while the Dutch had spirited away coffee seedlings from the Arabian peninsula, and were growing coffee on Java in 1696, there is no mention of coffee at the Hortus until 1701, while nutmeg shows up the following year. By then the Dutch had grown rich from cornering the market in spices, particularly cloves, nutmeg and pepper. They took control of the Spice Islands, and then transferred the plants to other colonies which had similar climates.

From this center section of today's garden, the paths then wind southward, and, surprisingly, upward through a gathering of ferns under the shade of fine mature trees. The small hill once formed part of the city's fortifications and is man-made. Leiden was originally built on islands in the Rhine flood plain. On one of them stands the *Burcht* or Castle, a fortification

Japanese cartoon of Philip Franz Balthasar von Siebold (1796-1866).
He spent six years on Deshima Island in Nagasaki Bay collecting
specimens and learning about Japanese landscaping
and gardens.

atop a sixty meter-high (200 foot) mound originally erected around 1100 as a place for the populace to shelter when the river flooded. The Dutch have long since tamed the river, but traces of it are still seen in the names of two canals—the Oude Rijn and the Nieuwe Rijn—the old and new Rhine. And the countryside is flat, flat, flat since it is bottom land reclaimed from the river delta and the sea.

(The North Sea lies about five kilometers west of Leiden. In 1573, during the Dutch struggle for independence from Spain, William the Silent broke the first and most famous siege of Leiden by breaching the dikes which hold back the sea and sailed up to the city's gates. Holland still commemorates the feat with a national holiday October 3 each year.)

This part of the Hortus was acquired in 1816. Earlier, other parcels had been added to the original space. The first major acquisition came in the 1730s by which time the collection had grown to 7,000 plants on 1600 square meters (about 1330 square yards), with one half-planted in trees. That left about one-tenth of a meter (one square foot) available for every herbaceous plant, and it appears that the government was shamed into action by comparisons with other botanical gardens. One garden supported by the city of Amsterdam, had three times the space. At the turn of the nineteenth century, pressure for expansion was even greater, and once French control of the Netherlands ended at the close of the Napoleonic era, efforts to refurbish the Hortus culminated in a large purchase which quadrupled the garden's surface area.

The new section was designed in the English landscape style with curving paths and lawns flowing into forest glades. In 1857, however, the university decided that the botanical garden should give up part of the additions so that an astronomical observatory could be built. Today the domes can be seen from many places in the Hortus, and the road in front of the observatory building marks the garden's southern boundary.

JAPANESE GARDEN: 400 YEARS OF DUTCH-JAPANESE CONTACT

The western side of the garden is bounded by the Witte Singel, one of the canals which encircle the city of Leiden. The visitor who strolls along the path bordering the canal will soon come to the entrance of the Von Siebold Memorial Garden, a Japanese garden created in 1990 to the memory of Dr. Philip Franz Balthasar von Siebold (1796-1866.)

Many botanical gardens have Japanese sections, some quite beautiful, offering a window onto an illustrious gardening tradition. None of those gardens has the historical significance of the Von Siebold garden. It is a symbol of the unique relationship between Japan and Holland, as well as a monument to a quite extraordinary medical man and plant collector.

Only Portugal has a longer history with Japan than Holland, whose links with the Empire of the Rising Sun reach back 400 years to the time when Clusius was beginning the Hortus and Dutch gentlemen adventurers were starting to explore the world. In April 1600 the *Liefde*, a Dutch trading ship, drifted into Japanese waters. She was the only remaining vessel of five which set off from Rotterdam the previous year with the aim of finding a new route to India and the Spice Islands. While this beginning sounds inauspicious, it came at a time when the Japanese rulers were beginning to worry about Western influences. The Dutch were granted exclusive trading rights, and they were allowed to establish an outpost on Deshima Island in Nagasaki Bay on the southwest coast of the Japan's southernmost island. From 1640 until 1854, this Dutch outpost was the only channel of communication between Japan and the rest of the Western world. (Japan only opened up after American Admiral Matthew Perry sailed into Tokyo harbor in 1853, demanding that international relations be established.)

The Europeans on Deshima had little contact with the Japanese. They were not allowed off the island except for an annual ceremonial visit to the Emperor, and no women "except courtesans" were allowed to visit. Nevertheless at least three men posted there were able to do considerable botanizing. The first was Engelbert Kaempfer (1651-1716,) a German physician and botanist. Posted to Deshima from 1690 to 1692, he came across the gingko on a side trip to China, and brought the seeds back to Holland where it was first planted in the botanical garden at Utrecht in 1730. Another botanist, Carl Peter Thunberg (1743-1828), was one of Linnaeus's disciples. He was Swedish like Linnaeus, but he had spent three years in the Dutch Cape Colony in South Africa where he learned Dutch and described nearly 3,000 plants. Then he went on to Deshima, arriving in 1775. There he exchanged bits of medical knowledge for botanical specimens from the post's Japanese interpreters who were hungry for news of European medicine. He also looked for samples of Japanese flora in unconventional places; he reportedly searched for plant samples in the fodder brought from the Japanese mainland for the post's animals.

Von Siebold was the third botanizer, but he was interested in far more

A Japanese woodcut of the man-made island, Deshima, built
first for the Portuguese (1634) and later occupied by the Dutch.
The botanical garden is to the left of the main gate.

than plants. A native of Würzberg and trained in medicine at Heidelburg,
he came to The Hague as court physician to William I in 1820. Within a
short time he became Surgeon Major in the Netherlands East Indian Army
and traveled to Java, and then to Deshima. During the six years he spent
there, he collected not only plant specimens, but also learned a great deal
about Japanese landscaping and gardens. In exchange for medical consul-
tations, he was frequently offered objets d'art and plant and animal
specimens. Today his collections are found in several museums in Holland,
and the descendants of the plants he sent back are found in the Hortus
Botanicus as well as gardens all over Europe. Among the plants that he
introduced were several Japanese hydrangeas, hosta lilies, peonies,
chrysanthemums, and wisterias. His herbaria and other collections include
items which today are not found in Japan, and Japanese scientists regularly
visit Leiden in order to study them.

After his stint in Japan, von Siebold became involved with a Dutch
Royal Society dedicated to the introduction of Japanese plants. During the
next decade the Society arranged for hundreds of plants to be sent to

Holland. Then Von Siebold quarreled with the Dutch government and when the Dutch foreign office scuttled his appointment as diplomatic representative to Japan, he moved back to Germany in 1863. He died there three years later.

Von Siebold's contribution has, neverthless, been richly remembered. A bust of him has been on display in the Hortus Botanicus for more than a century. In 1990 a Japanese "dry" garden was created in his honor, designed by the Japanese landscape architect Hajime Nakamura and his pupil, the Dutch landscape architect Wybe Kuitert. A rock composition opposite a viewing pavilion symbolizes mountains from which water flows into a gravel sea. One large rock is Turtle Island, the symbol of long life, while a second is Crane Island, which represents not only a long life, but a happy one.

The Asian resonances continue when the visitor leaves the von Siebold garden and enters the first of a series of greenhouses. A great many of the plants in this conservatory complex are from Asia.

GREENHOUSES AND THE LEGACY OF EMPIRE

Not all of the greenhouses are open to the public. Several of them are used for on-going research by the Hortus's botanists and the Dutch National Herbarium, the Rijksherbarium. Other off-limits areas house orchids which in the past presented a temptation for light-fingered people. Today a few orchids are on display behind barriers. The glass cases also prevent the viewer from smelling the flowers, which can be a good or bad thing. One, *Coeloygne rhabdobulbon*, is said to smell like milk chocolate, but another, *Bublophyllum phaelaenopsis*, is said to smell like rotten meat.

The study of orchids has been an area of specialization at the Hortus. Expeditions around the world are still uncovering new species of orchids and bringing them to the garden to be studied. When they flower the plants are described precisely, then sketched and photographed, and the resulting work published in the journal *Orchid Monographs*, which is published by the Dutch National Herbarium.

The greenhouses also are home to one of the world's most extensive collections of passion flowers. The Hortus Botanicus collection includes sixty-five of the hundred species of passion flowers, most of which are native to tropical South America. These gorgeous flowers are said to have been used by Spanish missionaries to explain the suffering (the "passion") of Christ to Indians in tropical America. A ring of filaments forming a circle around the central part of the flower was likened to the crown of thorns or to a halo, while the three styles were supposed to represent the nails which attached Christ to the cross, and the anthers were the hammers which drove the nails.

The discovery of the plant in the sixteenth century raised interesting theological questions as people tried to puzzle out the relation of the New World to the Bible's world view. How could such apparently holy plants have been unknown until the voyages of discovery? Did their existence argue for a separate creation of plants in the New World? Or were they escapees from the Garden of Eden, and therefore signs that the garden from which we all came was somewhere in South America? The theological concerns no longer appear pressing, and today the plants are grown either as ornamentals or house plants. Some varieties are edible, and are cultivated commercially in Ecuador and Brazil for use in fruit juices. Other edible varieties, including the apricot vine or maypop, grow in the southern states of the U.S. The leaves are used in herbal medicine as a sedative.

The greenhouses are also home to a forest of Asian ferns, some of them almost miniature and others as big as trees. They house a wide variety of tropical flowering plants and a flying flotilla of butterflies at various times of the year.

To stroll through the conservatories is to be transported safely and effortlessly around the world, but the greenhouses were also safe in another sense during World War II. The Netherlands was occupied by Germans from 1940 onwards, and conditions were tough. Jews were rounded up (130,000 were killed, including Anne Frank who lived in Amsterdam), more than 120,000 able-bodied young Dutch men were press-ganged into labour camps in Germany, and food and fuel were in short supply. During the "Hunger Winter" of 1944-45, many people were reduced to eating sugar beets and tulip bulbs and some 18,000 died of starvation. The collections in the Hortus Botanicus were winnowed to the rarest, most important plants, which were kept alive in a greenhouse with a pond. That the spreading chestnuts and oaks which still stand in the center of the Hortus were not chopped down for firewood says a great deal about how much the garden was prized by residents of Leiden. Hortus gardeners had permission to pull a cart to the harbour twice a week in order to get coal to heat the one greenhouse. The trips sometimes ended in scuffles: one gardener broke his arm when he was thrown from the cart when he tried to keep people from taking the coal.

The greenhouses' basements have many dark corners, and a cistern underneath the pond was empty. For a good part of the Occupation these areas were used as hiding places for Jewish professors and students, as well as young Leiden men who were under orders to be shipped to German labour camps. The situation was even more complicated: the University's library, right across from the entrance to the garden, had been seized by the Nazis and was being used as police headquarters.

Canadian troops ended the famine in April 1945, bringing 150 truckloads of food into the country in the first wave of liberation. For this, and because Princess Juliana, the heiress to the Dutch throne, and her family were able to take refuge in Canada during the war, the Dutch government gave 100,000 tulip bulbs to Canada the following year. Since then the Dutch royal family have sent 10,000 bulbs a year, as a continuing gesture of thanks.

The visitor to the garden won't see any evidence of that wartime history, though. Leaving the greenhouses, you will find instead a souvenir from two hundred years before, the Orangery. It was built between 1740 and 1744 when it was impossible to make glass panes any larger than about 30 cm by 60 cm (one by two feet) so hothouses were basically buildings with many small windows. The brick building, like the one found at Kensington Palace in London, the nursery of the Jardin des Plantes in Paris, the Linneaus House in Saint Louis, Missouri, and in many other gardens, is set facing due south to capture as much sun as possible through the rows of glass doors. Inside, palms, citruses, and cactuses spend the winter. In warmer weather, the doors are left open until the temperature drops to 5 C (41 F). Many of the plants are moved to spend the summer in the square in front of the Orangery or elsewhere in the garden. This twice-annual moving job was done by strong backs and arms until 1960s, but now a forklift is used since some of the tubs weigh as much as a 2000 kilograms. The collection of plants in the Orangery dates back to the days when the Dutch East Indian Company had an acclimatization garden at the Cape of Good Hope, which is why big plants grown in tubs are sometimes called "cape-plants."

In the courtyard in front of the Orangery near the low greenhouses is the second oldest tree in the garden, a date plum (*Diospyros lotus*) planted in 1736. Near it is a ginkgo which dates from 1785. The Hortus continues to evolve—from the same vantage point, can be seen its newest feature, the Palm House, which was dedicated in the Spring of 2000.

In their history of the Clusius garden Veendorp and Baas Becking concluded:

> Looking at this small plot of ground, so quietly and unobtrusively situated in the centre of what was once the largest city of the province of South-Holland, one begins to realize that what this garden lacks in area, in dimension of length and of depth, it shows abundantly in yet another dimension—in time. The embryo— our Hortus Clusianus, of about the size of a small city-garden— seems to have developed against the pressure of the surrounding houses, streets and churches. Its vitality was boundless, before its steady growth houses crumbled and streets were demolished.
>
> And every square foot of its surface represents effort. If any garden has grown against—and in spite of—difficulties it is the Hortus (Botanicus)...

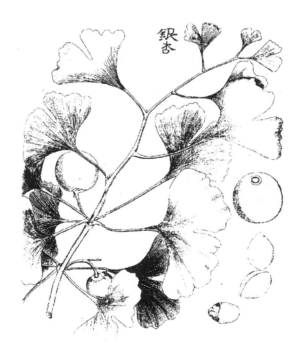

Ginkgo biloba.
Engelbert Kaempfer. *Amoenitates Exoticae*, 1712.

The gardens do not rank anymore among the largest or even among the more important plant collections of the world, where in other countries private or public foresight has created vast collections of plants.

The arrangement of the Gardens seems illogical and—perhaps—ill-conceived. But there is the charm of an old house in which not only periods of architecture, but centuries of endeavour are reflected.

We praise it as a Gem—let us hope that those in whose hands are given both forces—destructive and constructive shall share this opinion.

In the more than sixty years since this was written, the Hortus Botanicus has seen many changes. It continues as a monument to the curiosity of men and women and a tribute to their attempts to understand and appreciate the plants which cover our green planet.

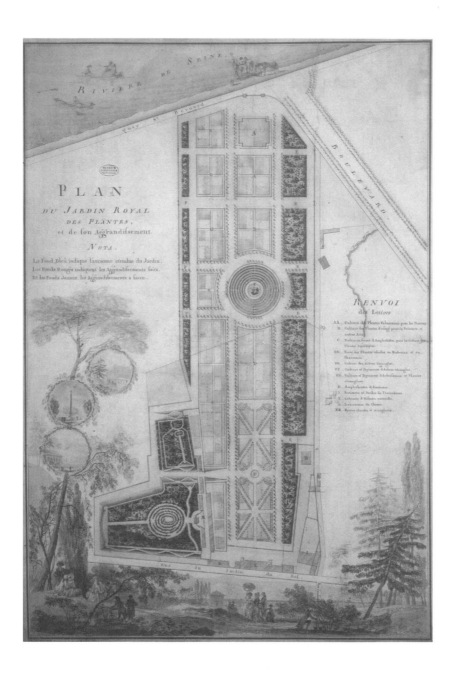

Plan of the Jardin des Plantes, 1726.

The Garden of the French Empire

AT 7:30 IN THE MORNING, when the gates of the Jardin des Plantes nearest the River Seine are unlocked, there already are clusters of people waiting to enter. Most have walked north along the Seine from the Gare d'Austerlitz, the terminus for commuter trains serving the eastern suburbs of Paris and the high speed RER subway lines which run north and west. They have fought their way across the intersection at the Pont Austerlitz, braving fumes from the cars and buses streaming into central Paris. Now they are ready to take one of the nicest shortcuts in the world on their way to work or class.

Nobody knows for sure how many pass through the Jardin des Plantes' twenty-two hectares (54 acres.) There is no admission charge, and no one stands there counting, but the best estimates made for the Muséum national d'Histoire naturelle suggest that in a given year, there are somewhere between six and nine million "entrances." That probably makes it the most visited botanical garden anywhere.

And botanical garden it is, even though the first impression is that this is just another formal French garden. A grill work fence runs around most of its perimeter. Inside the visitor sees grass, flowers, two double rows of trees, and broad crushed-rock paths running up toward a large elegant building a half a kilometer away. The vista is reminiscent of the one Le Nôtre designed for Louis XIV at Versailles with the Château at one end and the garden extending far, far into the distance.

The Jardin des Plantes is older than Versailles, however, and while it was established by royal command, it was designed to be a practical garden. None of the great gardeners of the seventeenth or eighteenth century attached his name to it; indeed the name of the person who drew up the initial plan is now lost. What its founders wanted was a place beyond the gates of Paris where medicinal plants could be grown and experiments conducted.

Royal Garden Dates from 1626

Standing amid the diesel fumes and the traffic noise today it seems hard to imagine that the Jardin des Plantes was outside Paris when it was founded more than 370 years ago. While there were quays and some commercial activity along the river, the shoreline in the years before the garden was established was sufficiently undeveloped for this stretch of river to be a favourite swimming place for King Henri IV (1589-1610). When his son and successor Louis XIII became king the neighbourhood was still bucolic, and a good place to find acreage for a future Jardin royal des plantes médicinales, the Royal Garden for Medicinal Plants. The availability of land was only one of the reasons for choosing this location when the royal decree was proclaimed in 1626. More importantly, the Church and the Faculté de médecine of the Université de Paris (located slightly to the northwest and only a short walk away today) would have no authority over a garden outside Paris proper.

It is more than just a bad pun to say that the Jardin des Plantes was set up where it was because of a turf war. Then as now, intellectual arguments and conflict of principle occurred in the academic and theological world. And then as now the spitefulness and pigheadedness among high-minded factions could be astounding.

The Faculté de médecine in Paris enjoyed the reputation of being among the best medical schools in Europe, along with Padua and Pisa. It had been among the first to take up the study of texts from the Greek and Roman greats when they found their way into Europe from the Arab world. Chief among these were the writings of Hippocrites (460-377 B.C.), whose influence we see today in the oath which every physician still takes: "First, do no harm..." Then came the writings of Galen (130-200 A.D.), who was born in Asia Minor, studied medicine in Alexandria, and served as physician to Roman emperors including Marcus Aurelius.

The rediscovery of these texts—and Galen wrote three hundred of which nearly half survive—made an enormous difference to European medicine. They were firmly grounded in Galen's own experience. He had occasion to study human physiology as he treated the horrific wounds that gladiators received in the arena. He used dissection of animals as a starting-off point for speculations about human anatomy. (Dissection of human cadavers was not allowed in his time.) He was right about so much that he was considered infallible by a significant portion of the medical establishment as late as the fifteenth and early sixteenth centuries.

But Galen was not right about everything—he had practically no experience with human dissection. His description of the human uterus, for example, is extrapolated from that of the dog, while he describes a system of blood vessels in the brain which are found in sheep and cattle but not in humans. His authority eroded as physicians tried to apply Galen's ideas to human bodies which didn't resemble those described in his texts.

The same thing happened as physicians and apothecaries in northern climates searched for the plants that Dioscorides described in his long text on the uses of plants. Obviously many useful ones did not grow outside the Mediterranean basin. Dioscorides never mentioned either the plants used in folk medicine further north in Europe or the plants flooding in from the voyages of discovery. These inconsistencies could hardly go unnoticed.

It took a fanatically-religious outsider, who also happened to be a brilliant diagnostician, to make a frontal attack on medicine based on ancient lore. Paracelsus (1493-1541), born in Switzerland and practicing in Basle, threw copies of Galen and other authoritative texts into a student bonfire two years after the Greek translation of Galen was published. Paracelsus was physician to many influential persons including the humanist philosopher Erasmus. The death of one of his champions and the storm his ideas stirred up led him to cut himself adrift from cities, and travel into mining country. The books he wrote about the diseases of miners combined careful observations with radically different ideas about disease. Galen, Hippocrates, and their followers over the ages believed that health depended on a balance in the humours—or fluids—in the body. Paracelsus believed that disease was caused by outside agents, and so his therapy was different. Not only did he believe in the efficacy of plants but he also tried various chemical medicines.

Paracelsus's ideas worked their way through the European medical world, and by the end of the sixteenth century his approach had followers in several medical centers. He provided a fresh theoretical framework for looking at medicine, which was compatible with evidence being presented by Italian and English physicians who had begun to delve more deeply into anatomy.

This more experimental approach did not interest physicians at the Paris faculty of medicine and the new ideas took decades to gain supporters there. For example, even though William Harvey announced his findings showing that the heart pumped blood throughout the body in 1619, the Faculté didn't accept the idea until 1672, fifteen years after Harvey's death. The following year, King Louis XIV had to intervene personally to overcome opposition from the Faculté and Parliament which wanted to forbid an anatomical "demonstration" of the circulation of the blood.

But at France's other medical school, Montpellier, physicians embraced the new ideas. A botanical garden was established there in 1593, and many of the faculty were interested in medical therapies using chemicals as well as plants. About this time, the King Henry IV placed the faculty officially under his protection, and from the time of his son Louis XIII onward, all the official royal physicians were attached to Montpellier.

This was a recipe for great rivalry. Montpellier, located 750 km south of Paris not far from the Mediterranean coast, was a Protestant city. This did nothing to make relations more cordial between it and the Faculté de médecine in Paris which was staunchly Catholic. Furthermore many of the Montpellier men also set up practices in Paris where they saw private patients, which enraged the physicians attached to the Faculté who were not allowed to practice privately in Paris.

The beginning of the seventeenth century was a troubled time in France. Henri IV, a vigorous and intelligent king who did much to heal the wounds of the religious wars which had torn France apart in the previous century, was killed by an assassin in 1610. His wife, Marie de Médici (for whom King Henri IV had built the Luxembourg Palace now surrounded by the beautiful Jardins du Luxembourg) ruled rather stupidly as regent for their son Louis XIII for several years. But even when the young king began to govern, most historians agree that France suffered from poor leadership. It was not until Louis named Cardinal Richelieu his chief minister in 1624 that the organization of the French state began to right itself.

JARDIN DES PLANTES

Richelieu, it is said, took particular interest in the developing medical theories, so it is probably no coincidence that in 1626, shortly after he took the reins of power, Guy de la Brosse, the *médecin ordinaire* to Louis XIII, received permission to create a royal garden in which to grow medicinal plants. The Faculté de médecine fought the project, and it took almost ten years to find the proper site, acquire seven hectares of land, and lay out the garden.

From the time it opened its gates in 1635, the garden was a place for free investigation of the natural world. Lectures and demonstrations were open to anyone. What is more, they were given in French, not Latin, which was a first in France. While the Faculté de médecine continued to be the only institution in Paris to award degrees in medicine, the Jardin (whose name over time was shorted to the Jardin des plantes du roy, and then to the Jardin du roy) became both a place for serious research, and a showcase where the world could observe the results

Yves-Marie Allain, current director of the Muséum's Service des cultures and responsible for the garden part of the Jardin des Plantes, says that from the moment of its creation the garden was set up to be independent, so that physicians and investigators would not have to conform to the received teachings of the Church. He explains: "The *médecin ordinare du roi* wanted to pursue studies on plants and animals. The aim was not only to study medicinal plants but to investigate the principles underlying life," ideas which were truly revolutionary.

Officially it was a *jardin des simples*—a garden of medicinal plants, on the Montpellier model—but the royal edict which set it up also named three demonstrators—doctors who were charged with presenting to students the "interior of the plants" and who worked on the confection of both herbal and chemical drugs. Thus what we would now call chemistry became a part of the program from the inception of the garden. By 1640 there were 2,300 kinds of plants in the garden with a "Cabinet du Roy" established for keeping samples of all drugs "*tant simples que composées*" as well as curiosities from the natural world.

And so began the garden which was to be the most influential in the world for nearly two centuries. At a time when England's Kew was still a royal picnic ground and Holland's Leiden, not much bigger than a wealthy merchant's city garden, the Jardin by the Seine was both a centre for botanical research and a collection of the world's most interesting plants brought home by French adventurers, scientists, and travelers.

One of the best ways to see the Jardin today is not to arrive by the Gare d'Austerlitz, but to take the Métro to the Censier-Daubenton station, and then follow the signs east toward the Jardin. That means you will enter the garden through the gates which run between the Grande Galerie and the four-storey house built by Georges Louis Leclerc, Comte de Buffon (1707-88), when he was Intendant of the garden. The Buffon house now contains offices and a bookstore specializing in scientific books. It is a fitting use, since it was Buffon who transformed the garden from a relatively modest demonstration plot into something grander.

Today the Jardin des Plantes is the name for the entire twenty-two hectare area which houses the main buildings of the Muséum national d'Histoire naturelle. Since the French Revolution the garden has been administered as part of the Muséum.

The space just inside the gates serves as the courtyard for the Grande Galerie. Built as part of the Muséum after the Franco-Prussian War in 1870 and recently refurbished, the Galerie now houses very popular displays about the natural world. On Thursdays it opens its doors to the public for a series of free early evening lectures which present the latest scientific thinking on such topics as the brain, evolution, and the cosmos. This public vocation is part and parcel of a long tradition begun with the garden: there are no diplomas given at any level, but the institution is still, as it was intended to be, a place for free inquiry.

GRANDE GALERIE AND SECRET GARDENS
The Grande Galerie is a favorite field trip for French school children. On a sunny midday, school groups will be waiting to get in, laughing and talking and filling the space next to the Grande Galerie with enthusiasm. The hot sun beats down on the stone buildings and the off-white paving underfoot. On the eastern side of the building, a vast white crushed rock expanse runs the length of the long Grande Galerie. Originally the demonstration gardens began here, but when the Grande Galerie was built more than 130 years ago, the first row of beds disappeared, replaced by light-coloured gravel like that seen on many promenades all over Paris from the Champs de Mars to the paths at the Tuileries.

If you find this brightness overpowering and un-gardenlike, remember that Paris is a city of garden secrets. The five- and six-storey buildings in the central *arrondissements* are built right on the sidewalk, so that the only greenery passers-by see is that of the public spaces: the centres of boulevards, the small parks nestled between buildings, and the larger horticultural displays. The buildings may be beautiful, built of light stone that shines in the afternoon sun, with details on cornices and around windows which seem to reflect a collective joy in the graceful and well-made, but very little green is visible from the street, even at a time of year when the chestnuts in the parks are hung with white or red candelabras of flowers, and the Paulownia on Ile St-Louis resemble mauve clouds along the river.

Yet often behind those walls lies a courtyard. Enter by a double door, and suddenly you are removed from traffic, from fumes, from passers-by. Around you tower the walls of the apartment buildings: usually six storeys high, festooned with window boxes full of flowers. And perhaps growing in the middle, a black locust tree, or lilacs, or a lawn dotted with flowers and surrounded by a graceful metal fence. An oasis where birds will sing when the sky grows pink before dawn. A surprise to delight the heart.

In much the same way, the grounds of the Jardin des Plantes are not what they seem at first glance. Through a combination of accident and design over several centuries the grounds have acquired secrets. They are not imme-diately apparent, but are neither hard to find nor inconsiderable.

So if you feel a little betrayed by the great white space in front of the

A white crushed-rock walk stretches toward the Grande Galerie.
Photo by Mary Soderstrom.

Panoramic view, 1860.

Grande Galerie, you should back up and start over. Right behind the Maison de Buffon is a delightful, if modest, garden which harks back to the spirit which animated the Jardin's first decades. The garden is a monument to Paul Jovet (1896-1991), "naturaliste, spécialiste de la flore française et urbaine," says the commemorative plaque. Future exhibits will feature pansies and violets, and, after 2002, plants of the Himalayas. When it opened in the mid-1990s, it was laid out in a more or less rectangular form, like Clusius' garden in Leiden or many of the physick gardens found in so many other places.

The plants featured were descendants of ones Jovet found growing by the side of road near his country house, and others which infiltrated the spaces between paving stones or cracks in buildings. Some of them are native to France, but others are immigrants, like *Buddleia davidii*, the "butterfly tree," which originates in China. Obviously it loves the Parisian surroundings, Jovet noted, as he documented how it thrived in waste places during and after the bombardments of World War II.

It is fitting that this pleasant and informative garden sits across from the Grand Galerie and next to the first row of buildings in which much of the research at the Muséum is being conducted. During the twentieth century the structures of plants and their genetic makeup was explored. Yet even as the building blocks of life are being studied at the microscopic and genetic level, the naturalist and botanist of the past has much to teach the scientist of today.

As a plaque in his garden proclaims, Jovet "incarnated a certain side of science, the tradition of which the Museum maintains: that of the naturalist who observes everything, with a sense of detail, all his life. From this viewpoint the most banal fact teaches much." The plaque adds that this approach is being rediscovered now that science is "confronted with the urgent need to inventory all the plants on the planet."

Straight ahead the visitor will see a living example of the fruits of this kind of botany. In 1747, Pierre d'Incarville, a French Jesuit priest working near Beijing in the court of the Chinese Emperor, sent back a packet of seeds of an unknown tree to his friend Bernard de Jussieu, the Intendant at royal gardens near Versailles. De Jussieu's brother taught at the Jardin, and some of the seeds were planted there. By 1779 a tree grown from the seeds became the first Sophora of Japan or Chinese pagoda tree (*Sophora japanica L.*) to flower in Europe. It now is the oldest tree of its kind in Europe, and has become a landmark in the Jardin.

(D'Incarville was one of many priests asked by French kings to send back interesting plants. He had arrived in China in 1742, but had difficulty in making botanic headway until he presented the Emperor with a native European specimen, the *Mimosa pudica*, or sensitive plant. This plant, whose filigree leaves curl up when touched, pleased the Emperor, and thereafter d'Incarville was able to collect many plants. Among them were the seeds of the delightfully-named Golden rain tree which he sent back to France overland by Russian caravan.)

The *Sophora japanica* is by no means the oldest tree in the Jardin des Plantes. That honour belongs to a black locust which is at least 150 years older, and is thought to be the oldest tree in Paris. While most other heritage trees in the Jardin are well marked, this one isn't, probably to keep the curious from threatening its health with too much attention. The tree's scientific name, *Robinia pseudoacacia L.*, honours Jean Robin who was the king's gardener even before the Jardin was established. Robin's son transplanted this tree into the Jardin in 1636. Today the lofty branches of the tree are gone, but the visitor who looks for it on the south side of the

Jardin between the Pavillon de Paléobotanique and the Pavillon de Phanérogamie will see the shoots it sends up each spring.

This area of the Jardin was originally intended to be an arboretum for trees brought back to Paris by the Jardin's naturalists and their friends. Robin's black locust is one of the few remaining trees, since this edge of the Jardin is now home to a phalanx of handsome buildings which house laboratories. In 1922, the Muséum national acquired 200 hectares (nearly 500 acres) of farmland near Versailles which were once part of the royal estate. Since then this land has become the Jardin's arboretum, where trees from all over the world are planted and studied in a systematic manner.

North Americans may think that Robin's black locust is not all that old for a tree. The Sequoias and bristle cone pines of California are up to five times older. Even in the Eastern U.S. and Canada, most of which has been logged once if not two or three times, trees 400 or 500 years old can be found in many places, including New York City. But the Jardin sits on the Seine flood plain which was settled more than 2000 years ago. (The ruins of the Arènes de Lutèce, a Roman stadium which probably held several thousand spectators, is only a short walk away.) While early records speak of forests as nearby, from the late Middle Ages it's clear that the land where the Jardin now sits had been used for the gardens of the Abbaye Saint-Victor. By 1148 the monks were diverting water from the Bièvre, a stream which emptied into the Seine upstream from today's Pont Austerlitz, in order to water their gardens. The canal, in fact, formed the eastern boundary of the Jardin until Buffon succeeded in acquiring much of the abbey.

Today the central part of the Jardin slopes gently toward the river, with the two double rows of trees accentuating the long prospect. In between are large beds planted with grass and flowers. There are numerous benches under the trees. On fine days hundreds of people rest there, enjoying themselves while children play in the crushed stone pathways.

Rose and Iris Gardens

Two special gardens have been developed to the south of the rows of trees. The first, just east of Bernard de Jussieu's Chinese pagoda tree, is a rose garden which was set out in the early 1990s. It brings together roses, old and new, fragrant ones and those whose perfume has been sacrificed for colour or shape. The story of how roses from China and the Near East have been bred over the centuries to create myriad varieties—a real romance

The oldest tree in the Jardin is the black locust (*Robinia pseudoacacia L.*),
named after Jean Robin, the king's gardener. His son transplanted
the tree to the garden in 1636.

of the rose—is told on placards.

The iris garden, a little further east, is smaller than the Roseraie, but its extravagant blossoms in May merit a leisurely stroll. At the far end the visitor will find a graceful, half-draped statue of a classic maiden holding a flower—Iris, goddess of the rainbow and messenger of the gods. Sculptures and whimsical structures, called follies in English and *fabriques* in French, show up on several early plans of the Jardin, but this statue is one of the few which remains. Massive, larger-than-life renderings of Buffon and the nineteenth-century naturalist Larmack, anchor the two ends of the long prospect from the Grande Galerie to the Austerlitz gate.

And in the middle, where fountains are indicated on nearly all the old plans, a piece of installation art sat at the turn of the twenty-first century— a grand sand clock inside a glass rectangle that reminds one of the glass pyramid which is now the entrance to the Louvre.

The rest of the central area is grass and flowers, although originally the beds were planted as demonstrations of different aspects of botany. As the emphasis in botany shifted toward work done in the laboratory, the more structured beds have been confined to the the École de botanique, a fenced-off portion to the north of the central area. There, 3,800 species are planted by genus and family for use in experiments and teaching.

GREENHOUSES

Just west of the École sit two large greenhouses which are open to the public. Visitors enter through the newer structure, an elegant tropical house called the Jardin d'hiver, the winter garden, which was built in 1937. All the plants here are younger than that however, because during the winter of 1945-46 a combination of terrible weather and post-War penury conspired to freeze everything in the greenhouses. More than half a century is enough to grow some large specimens, however, and this imitation of a tropical forest is now invitingly steamy and green. At the far end, the visitor passes ponds where turtles rest in dappled sunlight, and then climbs up through a cave-like passage to a second greenhouse containing plants from arid climates, which is sitting on somewhat higher land.

This conservatory, built in 1836, was one of the first iron and glass structures and is probably the oldest one still in use anywhere. Certainly the glass houses built by Joseph Paxton in England date from at least a decade later. Throughout the nineteenth century the Jardin's glass houses attracted crowds of people, Parisians as well as foreigners.

Among the locals was the artist Henri Rousseau (1866-1910), a retired customs collector who began to paint in his middle age. Without formal training he created large, intricate canvases, many of which portray tropical plants and animals in fantastic arrangements. "The Dream" and "The Peaceable Kingdom" are considered masterpieces of naive art, yet he never traveled outside of France. The Jardin's greenhouses were the closest he came to the landscapes luxuriantly full of palm trees and bromeliads, tree ferns, and exotic birds. Like Emily Dickinson, who said that all it took to make a prairie was a bee and reverie "and if the bees are few, reverie will do." Rousseau created the fabulous with what was at hand.

Visitors from the English-speaking world during the first part of the nineteenth century were clearly impressed by the Jardin and its wonders. Sir Stamford Raffles, who was to establish Singapore's first botanical

The Jardin d'hiver, constructed in 1937, has become a lush tropical forest since the cold, dark winter of 1945-46 when all the greenhouse plants died. *Photo by Mary Soderstrom.*

garden, took notes and arranged to send plants back to Singapore during a visit in 1817. Sixteen years later the Jardin provided the American philosopher Ralph Waldo Emerson with a moment of awakening in his understanding of the natural order. Nowhere in North America was there anything like the Jardin. Even in England, where many naturalists were at work (Darwin had set out on the *Beagle* two years before) Kew has yet to come into its own as a place of research. In the Jardin, Emerson saw nature as it

Abbé Armand David made three extensive journeys to remote regions of China to collect botanical specimens. He identified 52 new varieties of rhododendron.

was, beautifully and systematically ordered. In the following winter of 1833-34 Emerson gave a series of lectures on science which extolled his new appreciation of nature: "I am not impressed by solitary marks of designing wisdom; I am thrilled by the choral harmony of the whole. Design! It is all design. It is all beauty. It is all astonishment."

Who were the men who sent plants back to the Jardin to fill the glass houses and to grace the demonstration beds? During its first 150 years, they were not the Jardin's naturalists, for the most part. Many were sea captains such as Samuel de Champlain (c. 1567-1635), who brought seeds and plants from his Canadian voyages, including the fall aster *Aster cordifolius,* which Champlain apparently gave to Jean and Vespasien Robin to grow in their garden. Louis XIV instituted the practice of giving missionaries like Pierre d'Incarville royal commissions to gather and send back plants and seeds. One of the first was Charles Plumier (1646-1706), after whom the fragrant-flowered genus Plumeria is named. He traveled widely in the Caribbean and Central America, making thousands of drawings and leaving even more descriptions of plants. A hundred years later Abbé Armand David (1826-1900) collected the seeds of some marvelous plants from China. In addition to the butterfly bush which you can see in Paul Jovet's little garden, he identified fifty-two new varieties of rhododendron, and more than forty primulas. (He also described more than sixty-three species of wild animals and sixty-five species of birds which had not previously been described by zoologists.)

There was a practical reason to enlist missionaries. Their work opened doors to areas that would have been shut to ordinary travelers. But there was a spiritual one as well, since the discovery of God's creations was considered suitable work for religious men on mission to foreign countries. Most of the professional naturalists working at the Jardin, however, were content to stay in France. An exception was Joseph Pitton de Tournefort (1656-1708). A doctor, he was sent by Louis XIV in 1700 to the Middle East to study and collect plants, metals, and minerals which might be useful in medicine. For two years he traveled as far as the Greek islands, Turkey, and Mount Ararat in Armenia, bringing back 1400 dried specimens and many seeds. Among them were pistachio nuts which were planted about 1702 in the part of the garden which is now the Jardin alpin. The tree is still there.

JARDIN ALPIN

The Jardin alpin itself now lies just across the promenade from the greenhouses, with entry through the École botanique. The visitor passes neatly laid out beds where plants are grown according to their botanical classification, then turns north to go through an underpass which leads to the hollow where plants are grown according to their habitat.

The space was originally used as the nursery for plants to be eventually planted elsewhere in the Jardin, and as home for plants requiring special care. When a glass house which protected the most delicate fell to ruin in the 1920s, this picturesque ravine was transformed into a garden where plants found in the various mountain regions of the world would be grown together in more or less natural settings. The resulting Jardin Alpin is one of the joys of the Jardin des Plantes. It is a carefully laid out area where sun and shade intermingle and different types of soil have been carefully recreated. The pistachio, which from a geobotanical point of view does not belong there, nevertheless thrives. When the plant was young, one of the great debates among naturalists was over whether plants were sexual beings. There never had been any question that animals had sex. "Male and female, created He them," says the Bible. The reproduction of plants puzzled botanists for some time, until botanists looked closely at flowers and discovered structures which are analogous to male and female sexual organs in animals.

Years before Linnaeus published his ground-breaking work, Sebastien Vaillant (1669-1722) became convinced of the sexual nature of plant reproduction with some plants having definite male and female forms. The pistachio tree in the Jardin, he decided, was a male tree, which would never produce nuts. Another one of the seedlings had been planted about ten minutes walk away in the garden of the Order of Apothecaries, and Vaillant believed that it was female. So in the spring of 1715 he pollinated the flowers

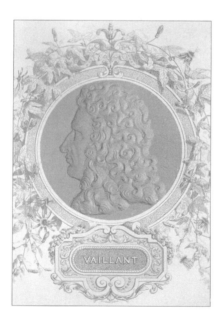

In 1715 Sebastien Vaillant demonstrated that plants reproduce sexually by pollinating a female pistachio tree with pollen from the Jardin's male pistachio.

of the female tree, and voilà, the female tree bore fruit. This elegant proof of plants' sexuality placed him at odds with the person responsible for the pistachios being planted. Tournefort steadfastly held to the belief that plant reproduction could not be compared to sexual reproduction in animals. This opposition may have affected Vaillant's career. At his death, his book on French flora remained unpublished until Boerhaave, Linnaeus's friend at Leiden, paid the printer. It was published in 1727.

Another naturalist who went plant-hunting was Bernard de Jussieu's nephew Joseph, (1706-1779), who travelled to South America with four other scientists to measure the degree of meridian near the Equator in 1735. They brought back the first cinchona seedlings, as well as descriptions of how the Indians had extracted quinine from tree's bark as a cure for malaria.

We tend to think of malaria as a tropical disease but it was common in Europe then, and no effective remedy existed in the Old World. Europeans did not learn about quinona until the early seventeenth century when the Spaniards encountered it in the Inca empire of the Andes. Legend has it that the Countess of Chincon, wife of the Spanish viceroy in Peru, was cured of malaria in 1638. In the following years, some of the compound crossed the ocean where it commanded immense sums. By 1658 it was advertised in England, and in 1677, it was listed in the London *Pharmacopoeia*. Four years later an English physician used it to cure the twenty-year-old Grand Dauphin, eldest son of Louis XIV and heir to the French throne, for the enormous a fee of 3,000 louis d'or. The "Jesuits' powder" (which it was frequently called because the Jesuits used it widely) rapidly became a standard, if expensive, part of the European physician's medical kit, although the active ingredients weren't isolated until 1820. The plants which de Jussieu brought back to the Jardin in Paris didn't survive, so the price of quinine remained high until the turn of the nineteenth century when both the British and Dutch used seeds smuggled from South America to establish plantations in their Southeast Asian colonies.

It was clear that casting the widest net possible paid off when collecting plants was concerned. By 1726, all captains shipping out of the French port of Nantes were given a royal order to bring back seeds and plants from all their trips. The apothecaries of Nantes would forward the ones which looked interesting to the Jardin in Paris after allowing the plants to recover from the arduous sea voyage in a botanic garden in that city.

About the same time, the first of the French colonial botanical gardens was set up at Pamplemousse on Mauritius, an island in the Indian Ocean. It was used as a provisioning stop as well as a way station for plants bound for France. Pierre Poivre (1719-1786), intendant at Pamplemousse, also effectively broke the Dutch monopoly on cloves and nutmeg from the Spice Islands by growing the trees in the garden. Other botanical gardens were established including those at Réunion, also in the Indian Ocean, and Martinique in the Caribbean.

The French had better luck with many other plants than they did with quinine. Coffee is a case in point. It is not native to the New World, but it was not until the Late Renaissance that it made its way to Europe from the Muslim world where it had been discovered. The first "café" opened in Paris in 1702, but by then the Dutch had already developed a taste for it. They had been able to finagle seedlings from the Arab coffee fields in Yemen, and by 1690 were growing the crop in their colony on the island of Java. (Mocha, by the way, was the Yemeni port, now blocked by a sandbar, from which coffee was exported.)

The Dutch and Arab stranglehold on the coffee trade did not last long. After the Peace of Utrecht in 1714, Louis XIV obtained a plant from the burgermeister of Amsterdam and sent it to the Jardin. The intendent had the Jardin's first heated greenhouse constructed for it, where it thrived. By 1721 enough new plants had been propagated to risk sending the first offspring to the botanical garden at Martinique in hopes that the plants could be established in the French possessions around the Caribbean. The coffee plantations of the French Antilles and French Guyana were all descendants from that one coffee tree.

As the century wore on, more French naturalists set out on voyages of discovery. Philippe Commerson (1727-73) sailed with Louis-Antoine Bougainville (1729-1811) on his trips around the world; the lovely scarlet, orange, or mauve climbing vine bougainvillea, native to South America, is named after the expedition's captain. André Michaux (1746-1806) spent twelve years in North America, travelling from the Carolinas to Hudson Bay. His son François-André (1770-1855) joined him for his second trip to North America, and the two set up a garden in South Carolina to prepare specimen plants to send back to France. Most of them did not make it since the ship in which André Michaux returned was wrecked off the coast

The Maison Buffon (next to the Paul Jovet garden), was built by
Georges Louis Leclerc, Comte de Buffon (1707-88), when he
was Intendant of the garden.
Photo by Mary Soderstrom.

of Holland. He survived and was able to save his herbarium samples, and they made it to the Jardin safely even though he was never able to catalogue them properly.

By the end of the eighteenth century, the Jardin's reputation as the place to prepare for an expedition was firmly established. The German explorer Alexander von Humboldt, who spent four years exploring South American and the western coast of North America, prepared for his voyage at the Jardin. From 1819 onward, the Jardin ran a school for explorers, with a handbook called *Instructions pour les voyageurs et pour les employés dans les colonies sur la manière de recueiller, de conserver et d'envoyer les objets d'histoire naturelle.* It went through four editions.

JARDIN DU ROY BECOMES THE JARDIN DES PLANTES

By then the Jardin was no longer the Jardin du Roy, but the Jardin des Plantes *tout court.* The brilliant Comte Buffon had led the Jardin through forty years of the eighteenth century, more than tripling the size of the grounds and adroitly encouraging research, all the while working on his thirty-six volume *Histoire naturelle.* He died in 1788, a year before the

French Revolution.

During that great seismic shakeup of French society, the Jardin's long tradition of free inquiry served it in good stead. Of all French academic institutions, only the Jardin and the Collège Royal survived the Revolution intact, largely because each existed on the fringes of the Ancien régime.

The Collège, which had been an intellectual counterweight to the Sorbonne in many ways, became the Collège de France, while the Jardin became part of a new institution, the Muséum national d'Histoire naturelle. Here the collections of curiosities put together by many of the French nobility were deposited after they were confiscated. These included botanical illustrations and dried plants, which greatly enriched the Jardin's resources. After the Revolution animals from several private zoos were also taken to the Jardin, where they formed the Ménagerie. The small zoo to this day delights Parisians, and occupies about a quarter of the Jardin's territory.

The Jardin did not come through other events in France's history with the same luck. During the uprising which followed France's defeat in the Franco-Prussian War in 1870, the area around the Jardin was under siege, and bombardment extensively damaged the glass houses. The surrounding neighbourhood was cut off from supplies for several weeks and the ménagerie animals were slaughtered for food.

During the Nazi occupation, one of the bears had the temerity to put on the hat of a Nazi officer when it fell into his grotto. The officer ordered the animal killed and the grotto eliminated. After the War the piece of land became part of the Jardin alpin.

On balance, the Jardin has fared remarkably well throughout its long history. Yves-Marie Allain, the current director of the Service des cultures, proudly notes that it is perhaps the only garden established in the sixteenth or seventeenth century which has been able to carry on an expanding program of science as the city grew up around it. The Chelsea Physick Garden in London had similar origins, he points out, but could not be expanded, leaving the field open for the Royal Garden at suburban Kew to become the foremost botanical garden in England.

At the beginning of the new millennium the Muséum national d'Histoire naturelle is reflecting on its future. Allain says that it is well-funded by the French government. Hundreds of visiting scholars collaborate each year with French scientists and the Jardin is deeply involved in research into biodiversity and actively promotes safeguarding our world's green resources. It is undertaking a ten-year plan to renovate its buildings. Its main vocation—to promote knowledge—will not change.

There may be a return to the Jardin's roots when it comes to the physical layout. Grass and floral *parterres* have replaced many of the beds planted according to scientific principles. In the future more space may be devoted to beds that will demonstrate scientific ideas.

"The challenge and aim is to make the visitor's first impression one of entering a garden where science reigns," Allain says. "People should realize that this isn't the neighbourhood park for the 5^e *arrondissement*, but that it is a scientific garden."

As it has been for centuries, as it will be in the future.

The Palm House.
Illustrated London News, 1852.

The Garden of the British Empire

IF YOU STAND on the southern banks of the River Thames, upstream a few minutes walk from Kew Bridge, you are about 14 km (9 miles) as the crow flies from London Bridge, but you would never know it. Willows hang out over the water, a footpath tops the levee at the edge of an old barge canal, ducks scrabble about in the water plants growing along the shore. It is not difficult to imagine yourself back in the days of Henry VIII or his illustrious daughter Elizabeth I.

The river begins a big, looping bend here, and in Tudor times courtiers found it a convenient place to disembark from barges which had carried them from London. Horses might be waiting to take them to Richmond Palace or perhaps they would walk to one of the summer houses built around the nearby village green.

Elizabeth's very good friend Robert Dudley, Earl of Leicester, held much of the property at Kew, and Elizabeth would sometimes meet him under a big elm on what was called "Queen Elizabeth's Lawn." Indeed, the antecedants of the Royal Botanic Gardens at Kew, the biggest and perhaps best botanical garden in the world today, are just as royal as those of the Jardin des Plantes—but in quite a different way. Unlike the garden of the French empire which was begun by royal decree for a scientific purpose, the first gardens at Kew were developed over nearly two centuries as pleasure gardens for wealthy landowners or summering members of the royal family.

Not much remains from that time except Kew Palace, also known as the Dutch House, which was built in 1631, twenty-eight years after Elizabeth died. That was in the middle of the Dutch Golden Age when the Hortus Botanicus was thriving, and the merchant who had the house built hired Dutch artisans. The house, which has survived the years remarkably intact,

Dutch House, built in 1631, is the oldest building at Kew.
Photo by Mary Soderstrom.

would not look out of place in Leiden.

The groundwork for most of what the visitor sees today at Kew was laid much more recently. Caroline of Anspach, wife of George II (1683-1760), was a keen gardener and devoted much energy and fortune in the early 1700s to developing gardens at Richmond Lodge, their country residence. (The line between the Richmond Lodge property and Dutch House runs more or less north-south through the present day gardens, and divides it roughly in half.) Caroline's approach was what is now called the English county style. One of her contemporaries described the grounds as "an agreeable wildness... that cannot fail to charm all those who are in love with nature." It was their son Frederick, the Prince of Wales, however, who first took gardening at Kew beyond the merely picturesque.

Frederick and Augusta's Garden

Frederick, born in Hanover, enjoyed the life of the English country gentleman. He played cricket on Kew Green and set his family up in a house on a property near Dutch House. There he and his wife, Princess Augusta, became avid gardeners, with the aid of a friend, John Stuart, 3rd Earl of Bute.

While the royal couple at the beginning were merely dedicated amateurs, Bute had studied botany at the Hortus Botanicus at Leiden during the time that Linnaeus had been there. (In admiration or comradeship, Linnaeus had even named a white-flowering American shrub after him, *Stewartia malacondendron*.) With Bute's advice and the royals' enthusiasm, the stage was set for the creation of a garden which would "contain all the plants known on Earth." Unfortunately Frederick's interest in gardening may have led to his early death in 1751. He took pleasure in overseeing gardeners at work planting trees and exotic plants, and his doctor said he died from "contracting a cold by standing in the wet to see some trees planted."

Over the next twenty years Augusta and Bute carried out their plans for the garden in a partnership which some said was far more than just a friendship. Whether or not they were lovers is impossible to know now; certainly Bute continued to have children with his own wife during this period, and would have eleven in all. What is clear is that with the help of the finest landscape specialists of the time they created much beauty on the sandy, not particularly fertile soil along the Thames at Kew. The botanical garden they laid out covered about three and a half hectares (nine acres). A few venerable trees survive from the period, among them a tall, graceful gingko that dates from 1762 (well before those planted in the Jardin des Plantes or at Leiden which date from 1780 and 1785 respectively.) Outside the botanical garden, several constructions appropriately called "follies" also remain: three "temples," which were places to sit and survey aspects of the gardens, the ten-storey Chinese pagoda, and "The Ruined Arch," an imitation Roman ruin. All date from the 1760s.

But Augusta, Frederick and Bute were not the first in England to bring plants together for appreciation and study. Oxford University tried to establish a proper botanical garden in 1632, just when attempts to set up one in Paris were nearing fruition. Indeed, Robert Morison, who became one of the most distinguished professors of botany at Oxford, studied at the Jardin des Plantes in the 1650s. A Scot from Edinburgh, Robert Sibbald, was studying at the Hortus Botanicus in Leiden about the same time, and returned in 1670 to start a botanical garden at the University of Edinburgh. The Chelsea Physic garden was begun in 1673, as a garden in which to grow medicinal plants.

Chelsea, Edinburgh, and the Oxford garden did not have Kew's

George III and Queen Charlotte strolling in Kew Gardens.
Engraving, 1787.

advantage—royal interest. The young man who became George III (1738-1820) had grown up at Kew. The son of Augusta and Frederick, he was also strongly influenced by Bute, who became his tutor after his father died. George III loved the royal estates on the Thames. His wife, Princess Charlotte of the German principality of Mechklenburg-Strelitz, felt out of place in London society and also preferred a bucolic life. They were to spend the happiest years of their long marriage in the country, which they transformed. George III put the Richmond Lodge and Kew estates into one parcel, and hired the greatest landscape architects of the day to redesign the grounds. He appointed Sir Joseph Banks, the explorer-botanist and wealthy landowner, to be unofficial head of the scientific part of the garden, with William Aiton as head gardener. Many people date the real beginning of the Kew gardens from this period.

These days some 850,000 visitors a year pay the £5 daily admission to the gardens, which is a paltry number compared to the three million who visited in 1908. There was no admission charge then and the railroad links to Kew Bridge station (opened in 1858) and Kew Gardens Station (opened in 1869) brought city dwellers on day trips to the most accessible country setting in the greater London area. The gardens were open to visitors as early as 1776, when George the III was about to lose his American colonies; the Richmond Lodge part of the gardens were open to the public on Sundays, and the Kew section, on Thursdays. There was a period in the early 1800s when visitors were discouraged, but by 1865 the gardens were open daily in the afternoons and that year more than half a million visited.

Visitors today who approach the gardens from the Kew Gardens Station side enter through a visitor centre which reflects the sensibility of the 1990s. A long shallow pond, slightly too wide for an athletic child to leap across, separates the garden from the waiting area. People are funneled into a modern building which houses a restaurant, shop, and meeting area where walking tours of the gardens begin. The stop for the tram tour of the garden is also close by; Kew is so large that it is impossible to see it all on foot in one day.

A garden is a work in progress, and the visitor is reminded of that when leaving the vistor center. Just to the left is a mural showing Kew threatened by wind. It is pieced together from twenty-three different kinds of wood salvaged after a huge storm in 1987 uprooted more than a thousand trees at Kew and 15,000 at Wakehurst Place, Kew's companion garden south of London in the High Weald. That storm was by no mean unique. In 1879 high winds and blowing branches shattered as many panes of glass in greenhouses as were shattered as during World War II bombing. (Kew was never hit directly, but windows were broken when V1 and V2 rockets exploded some distance away).

PALM HOUSE

Today the visitor first sees Palm House, the grand glass house which has become the symbol of Kew, from the walk leading from the visitor centre. It was not the first building at Kew designed to shelter plants during inclement weather. There are two older ones which still stand: the Orangery, dating from Princess Augusta's time, and what was formerly the Aroid House, first built at Buckingham Palace in 1825 and moved to Kew in 1836. The Palm House, however, has a special place in Kew's history because its construction marked the period of resurgence for the garden.

Sir Joseph Banks, the de facto director from 1772 onwards, was one of the foremost naturalists of his day. He took part in an expedition to Antarctica, and accompanied Captain James Cook on his voyage to the South Pacific during which Europeans first visited Australia. He was a keen observer and collector of plants who believed that plants from one part of the world should be cultivated in other parts. He arranged the shipment of breadfruit from Tahiti to the West Indies which Captain Bligh was carrying when his crew mutinied in 1790.

More than 7,000 exotic species were introduced to England by botanists recommended by Banks or his associates. In honour of Bank's contributions to botany an order of plants is named after him. Banksia are native to southern Africa and the "cone" needs bush fire to open so that the seeds can germinate.

Banks died in 1820, the same year that George III finally succumbed to the illness that had rendered him mad for years at a time. Plants continued to be sent to Kew over the next two decades, but the garden was rudderless. George IV and his successor, William IV, were not interested in anything more than the vegetables that the garden might provide for the royal households. By the 1830s the chief gardener, William Aiton, found himself responsible for all the royal gardens without a budget adequate for the job. Rumours swirled that people in high places wanted to throw out the collections and grow wine grapes in the greenhouses.

Captain Bligh cast adrift by the mutiners from *H.M.S. Bounty*,
April 1789, shortly after the ship had collected a thousand
young breadfruit trees. Note the two breadfruit trees on the deck.
Print by Robert Dodd, c. 1790

Breadfruit tree, native to the western Pacific.
David Nelson, the Kew gardener who accompanied Captain Bligh's
expedition to Tahiti, perished after the mutiny.
Curtis's Botanical Magazine, 1828

A committee was appointed in 1838 to study the question of Kew's future. It issued an ultimatum: either the gardens should be transferred to the public and given resources with which to create a first class botanical garden, or the whole enterprise should be shut down. It took considerable pressure, but in 1840s the government took control of the gardens, and Sir William Hooker was appointed director of the botanical section. Four years later, when Aiton retired, Hooker became director of all the gardens at Kew.

Hooker was the right man at the right time. Victoria had become queen in 1837, and she would remain on the throne for more than sixty years of great industrial and colonial expansion. England had lost much of its North American territory when the United States was formed in 1776, and Upper and Lower Canada rebelled in 1837-38, but after the end of the Napoleonic Wars in 1815 Britain and British mercantile interests found themselves with few rivals in India, Africa and the Far East.

It was a period of widespread interest in the natural world. Part of this was motivated by simple intellectual curiosity which could be indulged in a time of growing economic prosperity. Charles Darwin was only one of many naturalists sent out on British sailing ships, and in the 1840s he was just beginning to publish his journals of the voyage of *H.M.S. Beagle*. But in addition, natural theology, or the study of nature in order to reveal God, was a widespread philosophic current, having received its most eloquent statement in 1802 when William Paley published his *Natural Theology*. Hooker subscribed to it as did his son Joseph, who succeeded him as director in 1864. The elder Hooker supported exploration and scientific work, and made radical changes in the layout of the Kew garden so that God's wonders could be displayed and explained.

One of the first changes on Sir William's agenda was a new glass house which was to be integrated into a new vision of the gardens as a whole. The architect Decimus Burton and landscape architect William Nesfield were enlisted to work on the plan. Queen Victoria initially demanded that Palm House be placed so it could not be visible from Dutch House, but Burton's model of the nearly transparent structure so impressed her that she suggested it be placed in a "conspicuous position." Nesfield saw that it was, to the delight of millions. The main entrance at that time was near the Kew Bridge over the Thames, so he laid out the Broad Walk which extends from that gate almost to Dutch House, and then swings around at a right angle to proceed directly toward the pond in which the Palm House is reflected. Nesfield originally lined Broad Walk with tall Himalayan deodar cedars interspersed with flower beds and rhododendrons. His aim was to have a tunnel effect leading to the edge of the pond where the Palm House would dramatically appear. Unfortunately, the deodars as well as young Atlas cedars planted to replace them in 1913, and tulip trees planted to replace *them* in 1938, did not thrive in the sandy soil, so the effect was never realized. Plans now are to replant mature Atlas cedars along the walk in hopes that the trees, native of North African mountains and adapted to hot dry summers, will fare better.

The Palm House is a shimmering structure, seeming to float above the pond in front of it with its graceful metal supports painted white. Its construction owes its success to the development in the 1830s of processes for manufacturing large panes of glass, and thin metal to replace wooden supports. (The removal in 1845 of a high tax on glass also set the stage and the Palm construction was completed in 1848.) The new technology allowed more sunlight to reach the plants, so much in fact that to avoid scorching the plants, the original glass panes were tinted green by the addition of copper oxide during manufacture. Kew gardeners by the end of the century rued the decision because the air in the Thames valley became filthy from pollution from coal-fired industry and heating. After 1895, when green panes broke they were replaced by clear ones. As late as the 1950s, when the Palm House was refitted, the graceful, curved glass walls were a patchwork of clear, green and pinkish panes, the pink due to oxidation of elements in the glass.

The visitor reaches the Palm House by skirting the reflecting pond and beds of tulips in spring, and annuals later in the season. At the entrance to the Palm House signs remind visitors to close the doors after they enter. No matter how cold the day outside, the atmosphere inside is tropical. Trees and vines climb a cast iron staircase which leads to a catwalk around the top level. At the center, the Palm House is twenty meters (sixty-six feet) high. This height permits reproduction of the three levels found in a tropical forest where plants have adapted to take advantage of every available space, vertical as well as horizontal. A hectare of woodland in southern England might contain between ten to fifteen species of flowering plants, but the same area in a rain forest could be home to 400.

Conserving and cataloguing the plant species of the tropics is currently

The Palm House as it looks today.

one of the major policy aims at Kew. The garden is involved in several major plant inventory projects. One of them is a three-year effort to conduct botanical inventories in Western Cameroon. Another project concentrates on the orchids of Madagascar. The impetus for these and similar projects is to understand and protect the natural world. Kew scientists have a strong sense of mission based on the idea that we must be the stewards of this good, green earth. This is not incompatible with the natural theology so popular in the nineteenth century or with personal philosophies which make no reference to a god or gods and which are probably more widely held by scientists today. The stewardship idea differs greatly from another philosophical current popular in the Victorian age: that God made this world for humans to enjoy, so making plants serve humans was doing God's work. A corollary misreads Darwin's ideas about natural selection: "primitive" peoples in the colonies were incapable of looking after themselves, and so the British should guide, "civilize," and Christianize them, and "develop" natural resources. Transplanting rubber and quinine trees from South America to other tropical regions thus increasing the supply of rubber and quinine was considered without question a good thing. How doing this might affect local cultures or ecosystems was thought to be of minor importance.

That kind of thinking was prevalent during the halcyon days of the British Empire. As former colonies gained their independence in the second half of the twentieth century, however, it came under question, particularly as it became apparent just how much damage could be done by transforming former rain forest into one-crop agricultural fields. The visitor to the Palm House today sees over and over again the call for preservation of the rain forest that remains and for the protection and serious study of the multitude of life forms which exist there.

Heat to keep the Palm House at a minimum temperature of 16 degrees C (61 F) during the winter was originally provided by coal- and coke-fired boilers in the basement; the smoke stack was on the other side of the reflecting pond. Unfortunately, the boiler rooms were below the level of the pond and were regularly flooded, so smoke stacks and boilers were built outside the Palm House. It is now heated with gas, and since its restoration in the 1980s it has operated with much more heat efficiency.

The change in heating liberated the lower levels. A stairway leads to the darkness of the Palm House basement where the light emanates from four tanks which display salt water ecosystems: rocky shores, mangrove swamps, coral reefs, and salt-water marshes. The installation ingeniously imitates not only the complex balance of sea water, but also the rise and fall of tides and the energy of breaking waves. The sea is the habitat of two-thirds of the world's plants. That is a breath-taking thought, even more impressive when you realize that the single-celled algae living in the world's waters produce more oxygen than all other plants, including the tropical rain forests which have been called the lungs of the earth.

Grand Vistas

The Palm House's western doors open to the grand, ordered vistas designed by Nesfield. Directly in front is a rose garden enclosed in a semi-circular holly hedge with carefully-trimmed domes. The arrangement is pierced at three places. To the left, a wide grass alley leads to Princess Augusta's pagoda, about three-quarters of a kilometer (half a mile) away. To the right, a similar alley ends at a lofty Cedar of Lebanon, planted at the end of 1700s. In the centre a broad expanse extends as far as the eye can see on ordinary, misty English days. On sunny, clear days, though, you can see Syon House, the Duke of Northumberland's manor on the other side of the Thames.

There are fashions in garden designs, just as in anything else. George III's landscape architect, Capability Brown, aimed for a "naturalness" based on meadows and rolling terrain (he excavated the little valley which is now the rhododendron dell). Victorian taste harkened back to the formal plans of the late seventeenth and early eighteenth centuries when the great French formal gardens had been laid out. Standing at the western edge of the Palm House, the visitor can see similarities between this most Victorian vista and the view at Versailles, *côté jardin*. Louis XIV's grand garden extends into the distance. The landscape there, as here, is designed to lead the eye to certain features and to avoid others.

Nesfield, however, was designing a botanical garden and, in this portion of the garden, an arboretum. He and Sir William Hooker squabbled about the relative demands of botany and beauty. Trees should be planted in groups according to their botanical relationships, Hooker insisted, but Nesfield countered that "If we are thus fettered there will be immense difficulty in managing the artistic department, because high growth may happen to come where we want low or open glade and vice versa." It was only by devoting more land to the arboretum (Nesfield said it would take 150 acres—about 60 hectares) that these sometimes contradictory sets of priorities were reconciled.

The result is the pattern of woods and clearings that provide the background for everything that has happened at Kew since. Many of the trees planted then still survive, aged 150 years or more. They are responsible for a considerable part of Kew's attraction for the nature lover today.

Stroll down the grassy clearing toward Princess Augusta's pagoda, and the visitor will soon see another glass house through the trees to the right.

This is the Temperate House which is even larger than the Palm House. It is a series of five glass houses planned as one unit. The idea was to provide a sheltered space in which to grow plants which are "borderline" in Kew's climate. They originate from a wide range of places including the warm-temperate areas of southern Africa, Australia, Asia, Chile, southern Europe and New Zealand.

The first parts of the Temperate House to be built were two octagonal buildings completed in 1862. The largest, central section was completed the following year. North and south wings were planned from the beginning but weren't completed until 1898, because of lack of funding. The design had flaws too. Chimneys were so low that soot was deposited directly on the glass house window panes, and a complicated ventilation scheme, which involved windows rolling back on themselves, never worked. The house was formally opened to the public in 1898, but it wasn't until the complex was reconstructed in the 1980s that it became the effective place for growing and display that William and Joseph Hooker had intended.

Most people find the temperature and the level of humidity pleasant. Among the plants which thrive here are tea, citrus fruit, and olives, as well as the world's tallest indoor plant, a Chilean wine palm. Another remarkable plant is the oldest greenhouse plant at Kew, a palm-like cycad, called *Encephalartos longifolius,* collected in Natal by Francis Masson in 1775.

Also from Africa is *Encephalartos woodii,* a cycad found in Zululand in 1895. This plant—the only one of its kind ever found in the wild—was male, and three of its four stems were brought back by an expedition in 1899. Other specimens have been propagated from the shoots, but today the species only exists in botanical gardens. Kew's plant bears the rather sad legend: "As no female plants have ever been found, the seed cones are unknown."

The Temperate House is also home to a particularly lovely bird-of-paradise flower. The plant has been successfully grown in many places— it's commonly used in outdoor horticultural displays from California to Singapore—but it originally comes from Africa. This specimen is thought to be from the original stock introduced by Sir Joseph Banks in 1773. He named it *Strelitza regina* after Queen Charlotte.

She loved the gardens along the Thames, and had a cottage built which the family used for picnics. Visitors can reach it by following paths leading west from the Temperate House. In late April and early May the woodlands in this western part of the gardens are full of bluebells. Since 1999 a spring fair called Bluebells and Broomsticks has been held around Queen Charlotte's Cottage, which was given to the nation by Queen Victoria as part of her Diamond Jubilee celebrations in 1898. Traditional crafts, from sedge brooms to baskets made from wood cut from coppiced trees are on display, and there are guided tours of the cottage. But the biggest attraction is the woods where blue clouds of flowers floating over the green grass hint at what an untouched English woodland might have looked like.

CONSERVATION

While it contains a few exotic trees like the monkey puzzle tree, this thirty-seven-acre section of the garden is now being managed to "maintain, improve and create habitats for British wildlife." It includes a meadow which apparently has never been cultivated, and where ten different species of grass thrive, as well as a hazel coppice where the shoots are regularly cut down to the stump so that new branches sprout from the base.

The bluebells are among one hundred species of plants being carefully monitored by Kew scientists as part of a Millennial project to see if global warming is affecting the dates when plants at Kew flower. The project follows one begun in the 1950s by Nigel Hepper which kept track of the flowering dates of more than five thousand species growing at Kew. Unfortunately these records are not continuous, but the future flowering dates will be stored in a complete data base for easy analysis.

In the 1990s Kew increasingly became concerned about conservation closer to home. A survey in 1992 found that twenty-three species of butterflies frequented Kew, which was not considered low, but which could be improved upon. The gardens adopted a grass-cutting policy aimed at encouraging butterflies and native plants. Some areas, like the bluebell woods, are mowed every other year to allow butterfly eggs, caterpillars, and pupae to overwinter in the long grass. This practice imitates the two-year fallow and grazing cycle which English farmers followed for centuries, and favours the plants which were once common in the countryside. Grass

Bluebell.
J. Foord. *Decorative Plant and Flower Studies*, 1906.

in other sections of the gardens is cut once a year in late October or early November to allow late season plants growing in the grass to flower and set seed. Still other areas are cut three times a year to promote the flowering of important nectar-producing plants and the growth of plants on which butterfly larvae feed, while the rest of the lawns are cut no shorter than ten centimeters (four inches) to provide a suitable habitat for low growing wildflowers to bloom and set seed.

In the summer of 2000, this program of encouraging wild flowers and local plants was carried a step further. The long, wide flower beds along Nesfield's Broad Walk extending from the entrance off Kew Green toward the Palm House were planted with a mixture of wildflowers and native grasses. Many of these, like the yellow corn marigold and the magenta corn cockle, were once common but are now endangered. By late summer the expanse was a glory of flowers and grass plumes. (Earlier in the season, the seeds sown in the beds had to be protected with netting from the gardens' ubiquitous Canada geese—an example of an introduced life form which causes problems for indigenous ones.)

MILLENNIUM SEED BANK

Kew's concern about conservation has its biggest manifestation in the Millennium Seed Bank project. The £80 million undertaking is housed in new facilities at Kew's Wakehurst auxiliary garden.

Wakehurst was chosen both because space is at a premium at Kew and because planners were concerned about security in the main garden. It is located on the Thames flood plain, after all, and if global warming causes rising sea levels, the garden could conceivably be inundated. As well, Kew lies directly under the flight path to Heathrow International Airport. An air disaster could destroy a seed project there. Happily, Wakehurst Place is only 31 km (20 miles) from Kew, but is considerably safer. The former estate of Sir Henry Price, who bequeathed it to the National Trust, Wake-hurst has been leased by the Royal Gardens, Kew, since 1963. It is set in terrain quite different from that found beside the Thames—rolling hills, woodlands, marshes, and meadows. Parts of the estate were virtually untouched when Kew began its management. Now it is being developed as a great arboretum and natural preserve that complements Kew, and as the site for the seed bank.

The aim is to collect seeds from 24,000 species of plants from around the world by 2020 and to keep them in secure locations for later use. If seeds can be dried so that they contain only five per cent moisture, about 80 percent of them can be successfully stored at -20 degrees C (- 4 F) for up to two hundred years. The seeds will be available to researchers, conservationists, and scientific institutions without charge, but if the projected research should have commercial potential, fees will be charged with the profits apportioned to the country of origin. The seed collection effort involves scientists from Kew as well as the country of collection. Participating countries including Australia, India, Kenya, Madagascar, Mexico, Morocco, South Africa, the U.S., Burkina Faso, Egypt, Iran, Jordan, Lebanon, Saudi Arabia, Syria, Tunisia, and Yemen. A portion of the seeds collected are to be held in their country of origin, a response, in part, to the criticism leveled at the role botanical gardens played during the great period of European colonialism when plants were taken from colonies and exploited by Europeans without the country of origin sharing in the profits.

And as charity begins at home, so does the seed collection effort. By the end of 1999 all but 32 species of the 1,400 native to the United Kingdom had been deposited in the seed bank. What remained were a few species so endangered that even collecting seed could compromise their survival, as well as a few others which only flower and set seed infrequently.

The Millenial Seed Bank is a giant undertaking, and one for which the world will undoubtedly thank Kew in the future, particularly if the destruction of natural habitats continues as it has in the last century.

From the wildflower-filled woods in the conservation area around Queen Charlotte's cottage, paths circle back toward the center of the garden and meet the Thames. There you can gaze across at the Duke of Northumberland's bucolic estate and Syon House, his manor with the larger-than-life lion rampant on its roof. To the east is the broad green alley that leads straight to the western entrance to the Palm House. That is part of what you would see if you turned left at the western doors of the Palm House.

Victoria amazonica—A Co-Evolution
If the visitor turns right when leaving the Palm House, however, the first building encountered is yet another glass house. This one was built especially for the mammoth South American waterlily, *Victoria amazonica* in 1852. The plant caused a sensation when it was first described by plant explorers who found it in British Guyana. Its leaves grew up to six feet in

Sir Ghillean Prance, former director of Kew, displaying
the underside of *Victoria amazonica*, when he was doing fieldwork
for the New York Botanical Garden.
Photo courtesy of Sir Ghillean Prance.

diameter, and were strong enough to support an adult. Seeds had been
sent back in the late 1840s, but it was not until 1849 that the first plants
were successfully germinated. There were only three seedlings one for
Kew, one for the Duke of Northumberland across the Thames, and one for
the Duke of Devonshire's garden at Chatsworth where the gardener was
Joseph Paxton. At one time Paxton had served on the committee which
recommended Kew's acquisition as a public institution and would, a few
years later, help design the Crystal Palace, a glass and metal structure five
times larger than the Palm House which was erected in London's Hyde
Park for the Great Exhibition of 1851. For the meantime, though, Paxton's
attention was focused on coaxing the lily to flower, and so was Sir Willliam
Hooker's at Kew. What followed was the nearest thing to a race that you
can get in horticulture. Finally in November of 1849, the plant at Chatsworth
bloomed, and continued blooming about twice a week for almost a whole
year. Kew's plant bloomed the next year too, and once installed in its special
house, attracted about 30,000 visitors. The craze was not confined to
England; the Hortus Botanicus at Leiden succeeded in getting the giant
waterlily to flower in 1872, and kept one alive during the coldest days of

World War II when there was barely enough fuel to keep the waterlily greenhouse heated.

One of the oddities of the flowers is that when they are dissected in the wild, a specific beetle (*Cyclocephala hardy*i) is often found inside. For a long time botanists suspected that the beetles pollinated the plant but did not know how. The mystery was not unravelled until the 1970s when Ghillean Prance, Kew's director from 1988 to 1999, spent long nights standing hip deep in Brazilian ponds watching the flowers open as night fell and beetles flew in and out. He discovered that the beetles were attracted to the fragrance of the opening flowers, crawled inside to feed, and were trapped there when the flowers closed as dawn approached. The next evening the beetles, sticky from feeding, crawled back out as the flowers opened again, picking up a load of pollen as they passed. Then they flew away to repeat the process in another flower, and, incidentally, to pollinate it. Today the lily is treated like an annual at Kew, with seedlings started every February, and set out each May in the Waterlily House and the Princess of Wales Conservatory.

Probably the majority of visitors who enter the conservatory, which was completed in 1986, assume that it was named after Diana, the Princess of Wales who formally opened it and whose death caused such a storm of sorrow in 1997. Indeed there is a plaque in her memory near the southern entrance, but the woman to whom this hi-tech glass house is dedicated was the Princess of Wales who devoted so much of her energies to the gardens in the eighteenth century—Augusta, the wife of Frederick, George II's son.

It is a perfectly fitting dedication, although one wonders what Augusta, who placed the Chinese pagoda and little temples in her garden, would think about this conservatory, with its right angles and special equipment. It has no side walls, and much of the area is actually below ground for heat and energy efficiency. It replaces a hodgepodge of smaller, lower green-houses which displayed a wide variety of plants from many different climates. Now the Conservatory features ten different climatic zones ranging from desert through mangrove glades to rain forest. Temperature and humidity are controlled by computer. While there is some overlap between the habitats reproduced here and those found in the Palm House and the Temperate House, the visitor can walk directly from one habitat to another.

The conservatory also has a fine, if slightly frightening, collection of carnivorous plants.

Tucked away in this corner of the garden is a group of buildings not open to the public. The Jodrell laboratories are the heart of the scientific research done at Kew. Electron microscopes are used to study plant cells while even newer techniques for studying the genetic makeup of plants promise to reveal just how one plant differs from a cousin species. The Herbarium and Library bring together seven million dried samples of plants, hundreds of thousands of printed documents, and the collected knowledge of at least four hundred years.

Even the most prosaic of samples can reverberate through the lives of millions. As an example, the samples of fungus that were collected in the 1840s when a blight hit potatoes in Ireland. In 1845 Ireland had 8.5 million people and was the most densely populated country in Europe. During the potato famine which followed the ruin of the potato crop by a virulent blight, Ireland's population was reduced by half through starvation and emigration. Most of the 55 million North Americans who have Irish ancestors are the descendants of those sad migrants of the late 1840s. The organism which caused the blight, *Phytophora infestans*, still affects potatoes today. Dr. Jean Ritaino from North Carolina State University has been using samples collected during the blight and conserved at Kew as well as sophisticated molecular markers to investigate such things as how new forms of the fungus are produced. The question is important because new forms may be more aggressive or resistant to the chemicals used today to control the plant disease.

Cutting edge Botany

Kew botanists are involved in genetic studies of flowering plants that doubtless would have fascinated the great botanist Linnaeus even as they sweep away plant classification systems like his, which are based on differences in the physical structure of plants. Botanists are studying variations in gene sequences to determine how closely different species are related. While the new data agrees closely with most of the relationships suggested by the physical form of plants, there are some surprises. For example, the system places the Brassicaceae family, which includes broccoli and cabbage, close to the Caricaceae family which includes papaya because they produce mustard oils, even though they do not look at all alike.

85

Those are only two projects. Hundreds more combine the latest in molecular biology and genetic research with the abundance of living and dried plants that comprise Kew. It seems a long way from the garden that Augusta, Princess of Wales, laid out, or that George III and his Queen Charlotte loved so much.

Yet Kew Palace, or Dutch House is still there, with nearby gardens that conjure up thoughts of their eras. The visitor might be tired after touring the rest of Kew, but, before leaving, a stop at the Kew Palace is in order.

The building itself stands with its back to the Thames and its face toward the lawns that now stretch to the Broad Walk and the rest of the garden. It was here that Queen Charlotte died in 1818, four months after Victoria's parents had been married there. (Despite having fifteen legitimate children, Charlotte and George III had no legitimate grand-children at that point. Their three unmarried but middle-aged sons were pressured to take wives and procreate quickly, which they did; Victoria was born in 1820.) The house is not open to the public, but the small gardens (collectively called the Queen's Garden) surrounding it give a glimpse of what gardening—and life—was like three hundred years ago.

The formal arrangement of hedges directly behind Kew Palace.
Photo by Mary Soderstrom.

Directly behind Kew Palace is a formal parterre, an elegant, geometric arrangement of low hedges with a Venetian well-head and a pond at the center. Standing just inside a tall yew hedge, statues of five mythological creatures guard the northern edge. They were commissioned by Frederick, Prince of Wales, in 1734. The best vantage point from which to appreciate this part of the garden is the stairs which lead into the Palace. The landscape architects have created a view for the Palace's royal tenants as carefully as Nesfield prepared the views from the western side of the Palm House.

The Nosegay Garden is separated by a hedge and sits at a slightly lower level. Its name sounds pleasantly frivolous, evoking small bunches of pretty, fragrant flowers held by lovely ladies. The garden is filled with plants whose smells—and often tastes—are delightful. Reading the labels and the explanations summons somewhat darker thoughts, however. People carried sweet-smelling bunches of flowers because it was thought that bad smells were carriers of disease. The garden also contains plants which were strewn on the floor to perfume the inside of houses and therefore make them healthier places. The association is spurious, of course: germs breeding in bad-smelling places cause disease, but bacteria were discovered only in the second half of the nineteenth century. Nevertheless these plants, and the herbs for cooking and for making infusions which also grow here, bear witness to the Nosegay Garden's connection with medicinal gardens which were the direct ancestors of botanical gardens.

The Thames flows on the other side of the hedge at the back of the garden. This is a good place to end a visit to Kew.

To leave Kew garden by the gate nearest Dutch House, through the beautiful gates designed by Decimus Burton in 1842, is also full of symbolism. Other gates in other gardens demonstrate just how far Kew's impact extends beyond this corner of England. What began as a pleasure ground for England's royalty has become the centre of a network joining inquiring mind to inquiring mind around the world.

Gardens of the
Nineteenth Century

A view of Palm Valley.
Photo by Mary Soderstrom.

A Gem in the Tropics

THE TANGLIN GATES to the Singapore Botanic Gardens are handsome. The visitor on a Sunday morning, waiting to cross the many lanes of traffic in front of the garden, has a chance to admire them. No point in hurrying after all—it's hot. Take your time. Note the fine ironwork, painted gold in the center where it spells out "Botanic Gardens." The white-stuccoed, squared-off columns which frame the gates stand out against garlands of magenta bougainvillea and tropical trees in myriad shades of green. Then, when the traffic light changes, cross the road along with the families pushing strollers and carrying picnic baskets, the elderly couples carrying umbrellas, and the groups of young people headed for an outing in one of the loveliest gardens in the world.

Their faces reflect their anticipation of a pleasant experience—and, in a way, the history of this prosperous city state. Begun as a British outpost in South East Asia nearly two hundred years ago, Singapore is now home to people from many places in what was once British Empire—and beyond. The gate the Sunday visitors pass through bears witness to that varied heritage too. It looks remarkably like the main entrance to the Royal Botanic Gardens at Kew, in London, designed at a time when British colonialism and the quest for botanical discoveries were both rising tides.

The island city of Singapore sits just off the southern end of the Malay peninsula, 137 km (82 miles) north of the Equator on the straits of Malacca. To get from the Indian Ocean to the eastern ports of Asia—Hong Kong, Manila, Shanghai, and the Japanese islands—ships must sail through the straits or go much further south. Singapore is the second busiest deep water port in the world and several times more maritime traffic passes through the straits than go through either the Panama Canal or the Suez Canal.

The tides of the British Empire swept through the region at the beginning of the nineteenth century. When Sir Stamford Raffles and his men made landfall in 1819 they found evidence of a major settlement on the island dating from perhaps three or four hundred years before. The first British accounts describe a wall 4.8 meters (sixteen feet) wide at its base and about three meters (eight or nine feet) high which stretched from the sea to the hill closest to the waterfront. The civilization which built it had long ago receded, and the island was home to a few hundred Malay fisherfolk living along the Singapore river and to Chinese farmers working gambier plantations inland. (Gambier is used in tanning hides). The hills, valleys and marshy lowlands were almost completely covered with jungle which made it look like "one continuous forest" according to a contemporary account.

A Planned Community

In the early nineteenth century the balance of power shifted in Europe, and consequently in Europe's colonies. Treaties following Napoleon's fall allowed the Dutch, who had spent twenty years under French control, to regain territories in South East Asia, including the rich island of Java.

Raffles, who had been lieutenant governor of Java when the British controlled it, was sent to Singapore to set up a new outpost. From the beginning it was a planned community. He initially established certain guidelines—the Chinese sector to be built on one side of the Singapore river, with the Malay on the other side, and the government lands at the base of the hill which had been the centre of the ancient Malay settlement.

Today Singapore is the successful embodiment of what urban planners all over the world preached following World War II. Its 3.5 million people are housed largely in high rise apartment blocks that look like LeCorbusier knock-offs. At first glance the multi-storied blocks appear little different from the ones which were built as subsidized housing in the 1950s from Paris to New York, Toronto to St. Louis. The aim was to provide decent housing for people who couldn't afford it otherwise. According to architects and planners, change what people live in and you will change the way they live. What happened in the big blocks seems to support that idea, only the housing projects have usually become nightmares, not dreams fulfilled. One such project in St. Louis was demolished after less that 25 years because it had become unliveable.

Sir Stamford Raffles.

Singapore is an exception for several reasons. Heavy-handed penalties—$5,000 fines for littering, caning for simple marijuana possession, and death for drug dealing, for example—have been enforced. Dissenting opinion is often quashed. But also from the start a generous subsidy program gave people a chance to buy their flats, thus increasing their stake in maintaining the buildings. Fifty years after the start of the ambitious project some 86 percent of Singapore residents live in such flats, and 90 percent of them own the flat they live in.

Over the years the housing stock has been steadily upgraded, too. The first flats were tiny, one-bedroom affairs, although much better than the slums they replaced. Since then the average size of a flat has grown progressively larger until now the standard size is three or four bedrooms.

There is another reason for the livability of this city of high-rises—greenery. Even though the skyline shows one apartment block after another, at street level what you see in most neighbourhoods are trees and flower beds. For nearly forty years, the government has aggressively planted in all public places, setting out and caring for a million trees and nine million shrubs to date.

This means that by the time the visitor has reached the botanical gardens' Tanglin Gates, Singapore's green spell will have done its work. It starts the moment you step out of the airport into the steamy, but usually fragrant air. Singapore has twelve hours of daylight year round, adequate rainfall and an average temperature of 27 C degrees or 81 F. It is a city of boulevards lined with flamboyant trees whose branches bear ferns as well as trees, where streets are shaded by majestic palms, where heliconia flowers grow wild, and where flowers beds of anthuriums are three times the size of the one in your living room. The Singapore Botanic Gardens are both worthy of the city and a major player in the Green City movement, having provided the stock and the knowledge necessary to successfully transform the city into a year-round flowering bower.

The Tanglin Gates.
Photo by Mary Soderstrom.

The Gardens are far from the oldest colonial botanical garden, although Singapore's founder, Raffles, wanted to establish one from the first. He was a keen amateur botanist. His book, *The History of Java*, which included a long section on natural history earned him a knighthood, and the plant bearing the largest flowers in the world, *Rafflesia arnoldia*, is named after him. At Singapore he chose nineteen hectares (forty-six acres) on one of the small rises near the present day harbor for his "botanical and experimental" garden. The site was planted with one hundred twenty-five trees, 1,000 seeds of nutmeg and 450 clove plants, and the garden became the supplier of plants to Singapore's first spice plantations.

After Raffles died in 1826 the garden languished. Then, when the idea of a botanical garden again surfaced at the end of 1850s, its sponsors, the Agri-Horticultural Society, had to look outside the growing city to find a suitable location. In the end the site chosen consisted of twenty-three hectares (sixty-four acres) owned by Hoo Ah Kay, one of its members. He was a public-spirited businessman whose wife had an ornamental garden at their home which included the famous South American water lily, *Victoria amazonica*. A photo from 1877 shows the plant flourishing outdoors at a time when European gardens were struggling to get it to bloom.

The Victorians who planned the Singapore Botanic Gardens intended to imitate European conventions. By 1861 the Gardens had ring roads which were perfect for a promenade or a carriage drive, while a bandstand near the top of the hill was the scene of regimental concerts. There were roses (which did not thrive due to the heat and humidity) and other flower beds, in addition to a small collection of economic plants. To make something more interesting would require the services of a director who was a trained botanist and who had an interest in investigating the region's unique flora. To find that person, the Gardens' board turned to Kew.

Henry James Murton came recommended by Sir Joseph Hooker, Kew's director at that time. Murton was only in Singapore for five years, but during that period he established the Gardens' direction. He set up an herbarium and a library, started plant exchanges with other gardens, traveled throughout the Malay peninsula gathering plants, added eleven more hectares (twenty-seven acres) to the Garden's grounds for a section devoted to economic plants, and began investigating the commercial potential of imported plants. The first of these to be successful was coffee, which became the major agricultural industry in the region.

COLONIAL HERITAGE

It was a strong foundation, and one on which subsequent directors built. By the time garden writer Edward Hyam visited the Gardens in the mid-1960s it was, he said, among the six best of the hundreds he had visited, in terms of "beauty, extent, scientific service and economic service." Its future did not look bright, however, since Singapore had just left the Federation of Malaysia after several years of political wrangles which followed independence from Britain. "Cut off from the vast country it was designed to service and be paid by, (the Garden's) future is doubtful," Hyam wrote. Certainly it was not clear how Singapore, with no natural resources other than its port, was going to make a go of it.

Nearly four decades later the Singapore Gardens have, in fact, fared much better than those in other former British colonies.

The visitor gets some inkling of this as soon as he enters the Tanglin Gates. As at the Jardin des Plantes in Paris, there is no admission charge, but unlike that venerable garden, there is no officious opening of locked gates early in the morning. The Singapore Gardens are open from 5 a.m. until midnight, and, while the Tanglin Gates may be closed overnight, there are several other entrances where no barrier keeps people out when the Gardens are closed. Yet there is no sign that homeless people use the grounds as a place to camp for the night, something which has been a problem at both the Strybing garden in San Francisco and at the New York Botanical Garden. Nor have there been attacks on evening strollers, according to the Garden's director.

Just inside the Tanglin Gates a road leads along what must once have been a stream-cut valley. The visitor passes a marsh garden on the left, and comes to the first of the Gardens' three lakes. To the right, the terrain rises gently toward the top of a hill where the administrative offices, herbarium and library are housed in buildings which date from the nineteenth century. Take the path up, and you will discover why the three high points in the Gardens each have a cluster of buildings left over from Singapore's pre-air-conditioned past.

There's a breeze up there! Or if there is a breeze anywhere it will be felt first and most strongly at the top of the hills. Artist Marianne North, an intrepid Victorian traveler, noted this in her diary in 1876. The house she stayed at was "like all the houses of Singapore...on its own little hill, none of these hills being more than two hundred feet above the sea; but they were just high enough to catch the sea-breezes at night, and one could sleep with perfect comfort though only three degrees from the equator." (North made eight paintings during her stay, including several at the Singapore Gardens which she found beautiful. They are among the 800 of

The silk-cotton or kapok tree *(Ceiba pentandra)*
Photo by Mary Soderstrom.

her works displayed in the Marianne North Gallery at Kew.)

On the slopes and near the top of this hill are some grand specimen trees. One of these is that South American native, the Cannonball tree, *Couroupita guianensis.* Its seedpods look truly like cannonballs, and contrast sharply with its lovely orange and yellow blossoms which grow on stems sprouting directly from the trunk.

Another is the silk-cotton or kapok tree, *Ceiba pentandra,* a native of tropical America and west Africa. Fibers from the large fruits have been used for filling pillows, mattresses, sleeping bags and life jackets. The tree can grow to fifty meters (150 feet) in height and measure three meters (nine feet) around, sending out surface roots which buttress the tree against high winds. The specimens in the Singapore Gardens often are hung with ferns and bear native orchids like jewels growing from the nooks and crannies of the roots or the branches.

A little way down the slope, you come to a fountain donated by Singapore's Swiss community on the 700th anniversary of the Swiss Confederation, which was founded in 1291. The marble sphere seems held in place by jets of water. The structure could be a metaphor for the earth, whose balance also seems precarious.

As you stroll around the gardens, you may see school groups—the Singapore Gardens are a popular destination for field trips. A botanic treasure-hunt might be underway for forty or fifty English-speaking girls of Chinese descent in short blue skirts and white tee shirts emblazoned with the quote "To have a friend you have to be one: Ralph Waldo Emerson."

Or a group of five and six-year-olds from a Muslim pre-school could be playing games on a lawn: the girls bright in fuschia robes and white head scarves, the boys in smocks, trousers and brimless caps in the same fuschia. Their teachers, like many Malay women, wear the baju kurung, a loose tunic worn over a long skirt, with their heads, shoulders, and bosoms covered by a scarf, the selendang. But there is nothing drab about them. Unlike Muslim women in some Arab countries, they obviously don't construe the Prophet's words to mean women should dress in dark colours: their clothes are as beautifully-colored as Singapore's flowers. And late on a Friday afternoon two groups of teenage boys from a Boy Scout-type organization might take a tour of the National Orchid Garden; one gets the spiel in Mandarin while the other hears the same commentary in English.

(Instruction in Singapore's schools is basically in English, the language of government and administration. Children also take Mandarin, Malay or Tamil—their "mother tongue"—in school. The current ethnic mix is not likely to change much in the near future since immigration is strictly controlled. The ground crews at the Gardens, who are largely from Sri Lanka or Bangladesh, like the young Philippine nurses and nannies picnicking on Sunday in the gardens, have only guest worker status and must leave when their contracts are up.)

Amid the tropical abundance traditional features often found in a European garden do get a little attention, but with mixed results. A section has topiary animals, while the sundial garden where waterlillies grow is vaguely reminiscent of the summer display outside the big glass house at the New York Botanical Garden or inside the glass houses at Kew, Leiden or the Jardin des Plantes. The difference, of course, is that the plants here bloom all year round outside.

Splendid Orchids

A spectacular feature that is unique to the Singapore Gardens is the six-foot-high hedge of the orchid Vanda Miss Joaquim, Singapore's national flower. A natural hybrid of two other Vanda orchids (one named after Sir William Hooker of Kew), it was discovered in 1893 by Agnes Joaquim, whose prominent family was of Armenian descent and whose large house and extensive grounds were located in a part of Singapore now crowded with high rise office buildings and luxury hotels. Then, however, the garden was Miss Joaquim's pride. When she discovered the orchid growing amid a clump of bamboo she recognized it as something new and brought it to the botanical garden for confirmation. Since then the flower has become much loved not only because of its beauty, but also because it blooms all year round and is easily grown (at least in Singapore.)

But Vanda Miss Joaquim is just one of hundreds of different varieties of orchids growing in the Singapore Gardens. Orchid breeding and growing has long been at part of the Gardens' work, particularly since 1928 when Eric Holttum arrived from Kew to be director, bringing with him new techniques which made it much easier to propagate orchids. The area now organized as the National Orchid Garden on the western slope of the larger Gardens is home to more than 12,000 orchid plants including 500 named hybrids and 400 species. Since it is the only part of the garden where an entrance fee is charged ($S2 for adults; senior citizens and children under twelve, $S1) attendance records are kept, which indicate 700,000 visitors a year, of whom more than ninety percent are foreigners.

It is well worth the visit, particularly for visitors who have been frustrated at botanical gardens in northern climates where orchids are displayed behind glass or are otherwise out of reach. Here there are as many orchids as there are daffodils in Kew's lawns in April, or tulips in the formal beds at the Jardin des Plantes in early May. The danger is that the sheer number will overwhelm the visitor so that not enough time is taken to look carefully at the flowers. There are yellow orchids on bushes, and purple orchids in hanging baskets and white orchids set out in beds the way day lilies would be in North America. Big ones, small ones, extravagantly multi-colored ones named after foreign dignitaries who have visited the garden, and delicate pastel sprays which look like foam lining the paths.

At the top of the hillside is the former director's official residence, a fine example of colonial architecture with the first floor open to the breezes. Here information about orchids is displayed. It is a perfect place to seek shelter from an afternoon thunderstorm or to rest if you are overheated.

To the east the view is out over the tops of the giant palms growing in Palm Valley. The eye is tricked into thinking that the vegetation is growing level with the top of the hill.

Then comes the Yuen Peng McNeice bromeliad collection and the Tan Hoon Siang misthouse. Sometimes called the pineapple family, bromeliads are a vast plant family, almost all of whose members are native to tropical or subtropical America. About half of the species grow on other plants; many grow on the trees which line Singapore's streets so that a tree may appear to have two completely different sorts of flowers and leaves. This collection presents a dazzling variety of more than 300 species and 500 hybrids.

Ananas comosus (pineapple)
Emanuel Sweerts, *Florilegium*, 1612

Next door the Gardens are constructing a Cool House facility where plants native to the mountains of South East Asia will be featured.

In the afternoon, when the shadows are long, is a good time to stroll through Palm Valley. Anyone whose exposure to palms has only been in greenhouses or to the sometimes anemic specimens that grow in California or Florida will find the experience awe-inspiring. Intriguing also are the sealing wax palms, a Singapore native growing in swamp forests and reaching eight meters (twenty-six feet) in height. Its waxy red leaf sheaths and petioles stand out against the green fans of leaves. So striking is the effect that the palm is now the Garden's logo.

Off the western side of Palm Valley is Symphony Lake, which takes its name from the bandstand on its north side which is used for concerts and other performances, and for picnics on rainy days when the roof keeps picnickers dry. But it is on the hillside behind, down where the lake becomes wilder, that the visitor will see trees to which the Singapore garden owes its reputation as a major force in the history of South East Asia.

WHERE RUBBER PLANTATIONS BEGAN

The trees are *Hevea brasiliensis*, rubber trees from the Amazon basin. How they got here is a story of great intrigue. How they changed the world is an example of what botanical gardens were supposed to be doing, according to nineteenth century thinking.

That many plants in tropical Asia, Africa, Central America, and Brazil contain latex had been known for centuries—Columbus may have been the first to mention "white milk" oozing from the bark of some trees. The Spaniards reported seeing bouncing balls in Mexico and recorded the games the Aztecs played with them, while the French explorer La Condamine brought the first specimens of *caoutchouc* to Europe in the eighteenth century. Within a short time it was used as an eraser for pencil marks. In 1791 the English-man Samuel Peal took out a patent for waterproofing cloth with rubber, as did Charles Macintosh somewhat later. The first mackintoshes were stiff in winter and melted in summer. In 1839 Charles Goodyear discovered the vulcanizing process which solved the temperature problem so that rubber could be made into hoses, driving belts, and rollers for industrial machines among other uses.

For most of the nineteenth century, wild rubber from the Amazon basin was the only commercial stock, although experiments were conducted with several other plants in Africa and Asia. Between the 1850s and 1913, when the bubble burst, fortunes were made by Europeans trading in wild rubber. So intense was the demand that a steamship line ran from Manaus more than 1,800 km (1,100 miles) upstream on the Amazon, direct to Liverpool, carrying trade goods one way, and latex the other. Ironically, it was a steamship on this line which carried the first *Hevea* seeds to be successfully germinated outside Brazil, which eventually spelled the end of the boom. In 1876 Henry Wickham, a plant collector engaged by Kew's director Sir

Joseph Hooker to bring back specimens, chartered an English ship to hurry some 70,000 seeds across the Atlantic. He got permission from Brazilian authorities for the transfer by convincing them of the need to release "exceedingly delicate botanical specimens specially designated for delivery to Her Britannic Majesty's own Royal Garden at Kew."

The ship called briefly at the French port of Le Havre, where Wickham got off. Then he crossed the Channel and hurried to Kew to tell Hooker about the shipment. Hooker in turn arranged for a night freight train to meet the ship when it docked at Liverpool. He had space cleared in Kew's glass houses for the seeds, and within two weeks after their arrival in England, some 7,000 seedlings had begun to grow.

Commercial cultivation, though, was still several years away since young plants had to make their way back to the tropics. Within a year, however, 1,900 plants were shipped out to the Perdeniya Garden in Ceylon (now Sri Lanka) in thirty-eight Wardian cases, the glass and wood miniature greenhouses used for shipping plants on the long sea voyages of the day. From Ceylon, seedlings were distributed to several tropical botanical gardens, including the Dutch Buitzenborg Garden (now Bogor).

Singapore received twenty-two seedlings, of which eleven were sent to other British outposts in the region. But the eleven remaining became the source of the rubber plantations that eventually covered wide areas of Southeast Asia. Henry "Rubber" Ridley, the Kew-trained botanist who was director of the Singapore garden from 1888 to 1912, is responsible for that. Not only did he discover a more efficient way to coax a continual flow of latex from the trees, he ceaselessly promoted their cultivation. Legend has it that he never went anywhere without a pocket full of *Hevea* seeds, which he pressed on landowners at every possible occasion. At first, he met resistance. Coffee was king of Malaysian commercial agriculture, and there seemed no reason to change. But at the turn of the century disease hit the coffee plantations just as the demand for rubber was about to skyrocket due to the increased use of rubber tires for bicycles and then automobiles. Those planters who had switched to rubber were able to ride the boom, aided by the fact that in the region *Hevea* was an untemperamental plant, growing practically anywhere and resistant to disease. By 1917 Ridley and the Gardens had distributed seven million seeds and by 1920 the Malaysian peninsula was producing more than half the world's rubber.

Critics of colonialism and the role that botanical gardens played,

Holtum Hall (left) and the Herbarium (right).
In the foreground is the single-storey Ridley's Old Office, built
in 1893 during Henry 'Rubber' Ridley's tenure as director.
Photo by Marlene Guelden. Courtesy of Singapore Botanic Gardens.

particularly in tropical regions, point to the rubber saga as an example of
how indigenous people were exploited to satisfy the demands of industry
in the more developed world. The Natives of the Amazon basin lost their
traditional ways and much of the forest in which they lived. The country
people of Southeast Asia were also displaced by the introduction of rubber
plantations. Similar disruptions occurred when cinchona seedlings were
spirited out of the South American mountains, nurtured at Kew, and then
sent abroad to be grown in plantations around the world.

After a good look at the rubber trees, the visitor can climb to the top
of the next high point in the Gardens where there is a colonial house at the
very top, and, slightly further down, a visitor centre which combines local
Malay architectural style with present-day audiovisual exhibits. A high dark-
timbered arcade open on all sides forms the entrance area. Big ceiling fans
make it a comfortable place to sit in the shade even at midday. A shop
features handsome crafts and books about the natural world and there is a
reasonably-priced café. (Food in Singapore, it should be noted, is excellent
and safe even in the open air arcades called Hawkers' Centres.) The house
at the top of the hill has recently been restored and transformed into a
classy, expensive restaurant, Au jardin des amis. That is a far cry from what
it was in the past.

SURVIVING UNDER WAR CONDITIONS

Officially the house is listed on maps of the Garden as the E.J.H. Corner House, and had been the residence assigned to the Gardens' assistant director. Corner was sent out from Kew in 1929 to fill that job, and he would end his long career in the 1970s working again at Kew. But during World War II he was one of those responsible for ensuring that the Singapore Gardens continued to exist despite the Japanese occupation. His memoir *The Marquis: A Tale of Syonan-to*, published in 1981, tells how the wishes of the Japanese Emperor, a keen amateur biologist, saved much of the scientific and cultural wealth in Southeast Asia. The Marquis was Yoshichika Tokugawa, who, aided by Professor Hideo Tanakadate of Tohoiku Imperial University and Kwan Koriba, botany professor from the Imperial University of Kyoto, was responsible for protecting the Gardens from confiscation by the military government as well as saving several scientific and ethnic art collections from destruction.

Corner's specialties were fungus and trees, and to do field work he enlisted original helpers—monkeys. He noticed how they scampered up trees to retrieve things, so with the help of a monkey trainer, he trained five who became adept at collecting field samples. One bit him in 1941 and he was invalided out of the Singapore Volunteers with an badly infected right arm at the time of the Japanese takeover. Not being in the Volunteers made the difference between being interned with nearly all the other English nationals, and remaining on the job where he had a chance to guard the Gardens' collections as well as other libraries and collections elsewhere.

The English population was interned at Changi Prison, close to today's Changi International Airport.Corner writes that he had to walk a thin line between doing what he could to get the Gardens through the war and collaborating with the Japanese war effort. His close relations with the Japanese scientists, many of whom he admired, caused tongues to wag among the English, but during the Japanese occupation relatively little was destroyed in the Gardens. Some of the worst looting had been done by Australian soldiers who had taken a stand there in the short battle for control of Singapore. The Japanese Emperor, long a member of the Linnean Society in London, had given orders that scientific collections were not to be destroyed in the conquered territory.

That order was not known to the Allies, and Britain was at war with Japan. The Linnean Society considered striking the Emperor from its membership lists at one point during the War, but did not do it, however. Corner recounts in his book how glad the society's president was when Corner told him after the War that Imperial instructions had preserved much scientific work. In 1971 on a state visit to Great Britain, the Emperor was elected to the Royal Society of London.

The close ties between the Singapore Gardens and Kew continue, although the last colonial director left in 1969. Since then directors have been men born in the region. In 1989 Tan Wee Kiat, a native Singaporean trained in the United States, became director. He led the Gardens through a redefinition of itself as a botanic institution and began a massive redevelop-

Dr. Tan Wee Kiat pollinating orchids at the Nursery.
Photo by Marlene Guelden.
Courtesy of the Singapore Botanical Gardens.

ment program. He is currently the CEO of the National Parks Board to which the Gardens belong. Chin See Chung, the Gardens' current director, is a native of Malaysia who was educated in Singapore and holds a Ph.D. in forestry from Yale University.

North of the Corner House lies the recently-redeveloped sector which once had been devoted to economic plants. For much of the post-war period the fifteen hectares (thirty-seven acres) was not administered as a botanical garden, but had been used as the site of the National University of Singapore and the institutions which preceded it. When the academic institutions moved to other sites in the 1980s the land opened up for a return to its earlier vocation. Now it is called the Eco Zone because of its emphasis on ecology and economics. Since 1995 as many trees and bushes have been planted in the sector as there are now in the mature parts of the Garden. So little time has passed since planting that the area still looks rather bare. Luckily several gazebos offer shelter from the sun.

A word about the heat. Summer days in the American Midwest and in Eastern Canada and the U.S. can be hot and humid, but in Singapore heat and humidity are constant. The visitor should drink lots of liquids (be sure to try the fruit juices which you won't find at home; soursop can be a revelation), and bring an umbrella for use as a parasol and as *parapluie* during thunderstorms. Evening, when the heat of the day is past, is a splendid time to visit the Gardens. Plans are to make night visits even more inviting with lighting which will put certain features of the plants in relief, echoing the very successful project, The Zoo at Night, at the Singapore Zoological Gardens. And because Singapore is Singapore, the Gardens are probably safer after dark than some Northern Hemisphere botanical gardens are during the day.

JUNGLE HEAT

To the south, past the visitor centre lies jungle where the temperature seems to drop by at least 5 degrees C (18 degrees F) as soon as you step inside.

Here are four hectares (about ten acres) of original forest, mixed trees, mosses, climbing vines, and other plants. A cloud of insect sound surrounds you, purer and more musical than the song of the cicadas of North American summers. Underneath another insect thrums with a beat that is almost like a bass line.

You might like to sit down to listen to this natural music, but there are no benches in this part of the Garden in order to protect this rare remnant of the original forest. Signs also apologize for the fact that the lights are no longer left on during the evenings so that the forest creatures are not disturbed.

The plants in this section are tagged with formal identification, genus and species all set out in a way that Linnaeus would approve. Informative plaques here, as elsewhere in the Garden, explain relationships between plant groups and provide histories of the plants.

The Gardens' current mandate calls for more work in taxonomy, cataloguing, and studying the wild plants of the region before more land is converted to plantation agriculture. For several years during the height of the "greening of Singapore" far more energy went into that project than into taxonomy and exploration. At the moment the Gardens are collaborating with Kew and other gardens, but the director Chin See Chung wants to do more. However, many young scientists from the region are more interested in high tech, molecular-level botany than in taxonomy. It is a problem that Chin See Chung and his associates are trying to find solutions to with some success, and with help from botanical gardens elsewhere and the support of the Singapore government which has been generous with funding.

But what should the visitor do in the midst of this reminder of the continous forest which once covered the region? There are programs to save what is left, and institutions racing against time to catalogue the rich biodiversity. They deserve the support of nature-lovers. But here you are, and you may not get a chance to come this way again. Follow the paths that wind through the jungle garden. Listen to the sounds, smell the many-layered fragrances. This is the original, this is what the Palm House at Kew and its many progeny try to imitate, but which can only be approximated in the temperate zone.

Savour it while you can.

Henry Shaw, founder of the Missouri Botanical Garden.

Henry Shaw's World Class Garden

IN 1820, while Sir Stamford Raffles was getting started in Singapore, Henry Shaw, the founder of the Missouri Botanical Garden, saw for the first time the land which he was eventually to transform into a garden. It was prairie then, and he was only nineteen when he rode out from the promising little town of St. Louis situated on a bluff on the western edge of the Mississippi River, just a bit south of where the Missouri River joined it. The half-day trip westward took him through marshes and past sinkholes and burial grounds, until he came to a high point where he could look out on the grasslands. He later described it as "uncultivated, without trees or fences, but covered with tall luxuriant grass, undulated by the gentle breeze of spring." It appears to have been love at first sight. Within a few years, the young man from Sheffield, England's steel capital, had made a fortune selling hardware and tools. He retired at thirty-nine and bought this land with the intention of building a country house and creating a botanic garden for the enjoyment and edification of his fellow citizens.

Fly into St. Louis today expecting to see grasslands like those Shaw saw, and you will be disappointed. The city, with its skyscrapers, housing developments, and railway lines, looks as you might expect, but what is surprising is the number of trees. St. Louis, to be sure, was the gateway to the West. The expedition led by Merriweather Lewis and William Clark left from here in May 1804 on its way to explore the Louisiana Purchase, that quarter of a continent that the U.S. had just bought from France. (French botanist André Michaux, who sent back so many plants to the Jardin des Plantes, was to have been a part of the expedition but was prevented from going at the last minute). Thirty years later, St. Louis was the starting point for emigrants, who would either follow the Missouri west and north, or set off by covered wagon or handcart across the great grasslands which stretched from St. Louis to the dry country at the foot of the Rockies. What is hard to comprehend, though, is that this ocean of grass was just as much a human artifact as are today's office towers in downtown St. Louis and the soaring Gateway Arch on the Mississippi waterfront.

FROM PRAIRIE TO GARDEN

Grasslands have universal appeal. Water is imported hundreds of miles to keep lawns green in California and Arizona, where native grasses grow for only a few weeks after the winter rains. In the forests of the North America's Northeast and Northwest people spend fortunes to keep trees and bushes from encroaching on fields and parks. In Europe the Grande Pelouse at Versailles and Kew's tree-dotted lawns are just two examples of the green expanses of grass favoured by Le Nôtre and other great eighteenth century French and English garden designers.

Some anthropologists and environmental psychologists think our love of grasslands hearkens back to the hundreds of thousands of years our ancestors lived on the savannas of East Africa. A number of studies done around the world have shown that people prefer trees shaped like those that grow on well-watered savanna lands. People also go to extraordinary lengths to have grass around them be it in the form of golf courses, soccer fields or parks.

Grasslands have been home to many societies. Native Americans thrived on the North American plains where they found game, wild grains, and other plants used for food, fibers, and medicines. In the area near St. Louis they regularly burned the prairies to eliminate young trees and bushes which would have otherwise converted the grassland to forest.

The result was the landscape which Shaw saw and loved, but which has now been transformed both intentionally and unintentionally. Instead of a city set on the prairie, St. Louis from the air appears to be a city set in woodland. Similarly the botanical garden's thirty-two hectares (seventy-nine acres) have been so changed over the years that trees and buildings are now all that can be seen from the lookout of Tower Grove House even though Shaw built it in order to see the Mississippi a dozen miles away. It is either ironic or fitting, depending on your point of view, that the Missouri Botanical Garden is a centre for research into biodiversity and a major

Henry Shaw standing in front of Tower Grove House.
Courtesy of Missouri Botanical Garden.

force behind the conservation of habitats and landscapes.

The garden that Shaw planned and paid for is one of the oldest botanical gardens in North America. He arrived in St. Louis just as it was ready to grow and was able to take advantage of the economic boom. When he retired he invested wisely in St. Louis real estate and then set out to revisit England. Between 1840 and 1852 he made three extensive trips there. If his timing had been right when it came to making money on the American frontier, it was also perfect for catching the enthusiasm for making gardens which was in the air in England.

Even as a boy, Shaw's interest in plants—and his good business sense—was evident. In a guide to the Garden which he wrote as a very old man, he fondly recollects the gardens where he went to school. Mill Hill School had been the house and grounds of Peter Collinson, a merchant and nurseryman who was responsible for introducing hundreds of plants into England. Shaw says he got away from the drudgery of studying Greek, Latin and geometry as a schoolboy by "growing pinks and geraniums, and retiring to a seat in a corner of (t)his little domain, shaded by a broad trained Irish yew, purchased from a neighboring nursery at the price of ten shillings."

When Shaw returned to England, Sir William Hooker was reinventing the Royal Gardens at Kew as a botanical garden for the world. Discussion raged about the necessity for a garden open to the public which combined a scientific mission with beauty. In addition, a number of great gardens were being developed on private estates, including Chatsworth which was just outside Shaw's old home town of Sheffield. The examples were there for Shaw to produce something remarkable back in Missouri.

The Missouri Botanical Garden opened to the public in 1859, the same year as did the Singapore Botanic Gardens, and Central Park in New York City, and also the year that Darwin published the *Origin of Species*. Shaw's Garden took up four hectares (ten acres) of the land he owned. The rest was his private estate, with Tower Grove House his country residence. Since then, the land around the house has been added to the Garden while the section of the estate immediately to the south has become one of St. Louis's largest parks, Tower Grove Park. Just as the botanical garden was influenced by Kew Gardens, the park was designed on English models with curving drives, gazebos, and many trees.

To enter the Garden today, the visitor arrives from the north side, driving through what was a fine residential neighborhood built early in the twentieth century, parts of which have since fallen on hard times. Pollution from nearby coal-fired industry was the first insult. By the mid-1920s the air was so bad that the Garden's orchid collection was suffering, and the well-being of the rest of the plants was also threatened. Through a complicated switching of properties the Garden acquired several farms about sixty kilometers (thirty-five miles) west—and upwind—of the city with the idea of eventually transferring the whole botanical garden to the site. The orchid collection was, indeed, moved in 1926 and remained there until 1958, but plans to shift the whole Garden foundered. Air quality in St. Louis improved because of new regulations championed in part by the Garden's partisans, and also because industry shifted away from coal. The result was a decision to keep the botanical garden in the city, but to create an arboretum outside of town. The 960 hectares (2,400 acres) of the Shaw Arboretum has managed to encourage biodiversity and natural habitats from wetlands to prairies.

But even though air quality in St. Louis is much, much better than it was 100 years ago, the urban fabric is worn. Like many American cities, St. Louis experienced a flight of middle-class homeowners toward the suburbs

The entrance to the Rideway Centre.
Courtesy of Missouri Botanical Garden.

The central hall of the Ridgeway Centre provides a transition
from the outside world to the gardens, and includes gift shops,
an art gallery, and floral displays.
Courtesy of Missouri Botanical Garden.

during the second half of the twentieth century. Many of the houses near the Garden were divided into apartments by landlords who have been less than diligent in keeping them up. To counteract this blight, the Garden is currently involved in an ambitious plan to revitalize the surrounding area. Working with four neighbourhood associations and with $1.5 million in seed money from the Danforth Family Foundation, the plan envisages new single-family residential housing, community beautification programs, and an aggressive attack on rundown property by putting up money for legal fees to protest building code infractions.

In the Garden itself everything is bright and well-maintained, however. On a spring day the parking lot is full of buses letting off enthusiastic and noisy school groups who have come to spend a day at the Garden. More than 100,000 children—whose ancestors came from every corner of the earth—visit the Garden each year. Henry Shaw wanted a garden that would reach people, and he and those who followed him have certainly succeeded. About 750,000 people visit each year, and more than 35,000 families are members of the Garden.

Spoeher Plaza

The entrance complex, the Ridgway Center, can hold a sizable number of visitors at any one time. Its architecture owes something to that found in airports. Visitors enter through ranks of glass doors at ground level, and then take escalators up to a great central hall which leads out into the Garden. Gift shop, art gallery, restaurant, floral displays, classrooms for presentations, offices, space for big meetings or dinners or formal events; the center holds it all, serving as a transition from the outside world. Few other botanic gardens control the visitor's passage so carefully. By the time you've made your way through the entrance complex and onto Spoehrer Plaza, you've been transported to a landscape that amazes and delights.

This is an entrance every bit as well thought out as Kew's grand vistas, but whose purpose is quite different. A fountain with water rising about five meters (15 to 18 feet) in the air lies at the center of the plaza. Brilliant annual flowers grow in pots or beds around it. Opposite of the fountain a row of trees offers shade on hot afternoons, and, more importantly, delays discovery of the larger Garden, whose glories will only be revealed slowly as you make your way around it. And in truth, what you are about to see is not one garden, but a number of theme gardens, each carefully thought out and placed to complement each other. They are set on a gentle slope, where a few hollows provide enough relief to provide variety.

To the right is the tram which offers a guided tour of the Garden. It is an excellent way to get an overview or an option for those who don't want to walk. But Shaw's Garden is not too big to stroll through in a day. Therefore, in order to savour the experience, turn to the left.

Straight ahead is the Linnaeus House. It was built as an orangery like ones found at Kew, Leiden, and the Jardin des Plantes. Originally it complemented other greenhouses which have since been demolished. With its long axis running east-west, its many south-facing windows let in abundant sunshine. Built in 1882 to allow plants from warmer climates to be over-wintered in blustery St. Louis, it is the oldest, continuously operating display greenhouse in the United States, and has featured camellias for more than a century.

It is also an homage to Linnaeus. Henry Shaw commissioned a bust of him which now sits high above the southern entrance, flanked by busts of Thomas Nuttall and Asa Gray, nineteenth century botanists who devoted their lives to the study of North American plants. Absent, however, is a bust of George Englemann, a German-born botanist who had already settled in St. Louis by the 1850s and whom Sir William Hooker insisted Shaw meet and take counsel from. Englemann turned down the job of director of Shaw's Garden because he thought it was located too far from the center of St. Louis, but agreed to advise Shaw. Among other things, during a trip to Europe he bought an herbarium of more than 40,000 specimens and acquired many botanical books which formed the nucleus of the Garden's library and museum. In 1999 the Garden's herbarium celebrated the acquisition of its five-millionth specimen which makes it one of the largest in the world. More than two million specimens were added in the last thirty years of the twentieth century, but Shaw had laid the groundwork for a first-class scientific collection from the very beginning. Among the very oldest are fourteen of the plants that Sir Joseph Banks collected when he shipped as a young naturalist on Captain James Cook's first world voyage from 1768 to 1771.

GARDENS AND FOUNTAINS

On the other side of the Linnaeus House is a series of smaller gardens and fountains: the Swift Family Garden of perennials, the Cohen Court, and the Baer Garden. This last is especially attractive, featuring as it does a fountain which includes a brass disk about one meter (3.25 feet) in diameter around which water bubbles. No jets bound into the air, but the sound of the water making continuously changing patterns is refreshing. What the visitor is also seeing here are two features which are found in many botanical gardens but which seem to have been brought to a level unmatched elsewhere: the use of water as landscape element and the sponsorship of particular garden features with the names of donors prominently displayed.

The Missouri Botanical Garden is still called Shaw's Garden by people in St. Louis It is, after all, the result of one man's public-spiritedness and philanthropic spirit, and as such it has few equals among public institutions in North America. Relying on the generosity of others to embellish the Garden is probably not surprising, given that history. The Garden now receives about a quarter of its revenue from a special district tax, but the rest comes from admissions, memberships, grants, contributions, bequests, investment income, and gifts.

Just south of the Linnaeus House are four lily pools. They are echoed still further south on the other side of bulb and rose gardens, by three more pools, two rectangular and one round. All of them are settings for sculpture, from Emilio Greco's "Bather No. IV" through Gerhard Marcks' "Three Graces" to the seven pieces by Swedish sculptor Carl Milles.

The ensemble of sculpture, ponds, and the Linnaeus House is visible down the long swath of lawn which extends northward from Tower Grove House, Shaw's summer home. In Shaw's day, the vista was a cousin of the grand view one gets from the Palm House at Kew. Since then the trees and bushes which he had planted have matured. His own mausoleum lies in a grove just north of the house. The prospect is not as commanding as it once was, but the axis remains an impressive reminder of the Garden's origins.

Because the Missouri Botanical Garden is older than most other North American botanical gardens, its stock of trees have had time to grow into imposing specimens. Nowhere is this more evident than in the area around the mausoleum. Shaw's pink marble tomb and "Victory," a sculpture which he bought for the garden, are shaded by mature oak and sassafras trees casting shadows that calm the spirit. The grove is set off from the rest of the Garden by a wrought iron fence, with gates at the north and south ends which bear a family resemblance to the gates at Kew's Main Entrance.

"Victory" is a nineteenth-century copy of a piece by Cosani from the Pitti Palace in Florence. Its pedestal inscription reads: "The Victory of Science over ignorance / Ignorance is the curse of God/Knowledge is the wing wherewith / We fly to heaven." This appears to have been Shaw's credo, although, notes the Garden's current director Peter H. Raven, Shaw was extremely circumspect about what he believed politically or theologically. His position on slavery and the American Civil War is unknown, even though he arrived in Missouri just as it was being admitted as a slave state into the American Union. Shaw also seems not to have been one of the nineteenth century Nature lovers whose appreciation of plants was a theological experience.

VICTORIAN LIFE

The entrance to Tower Grove House lies in a direct line with the path through Shaw's mausoleum grove and the vista toward Linnaeus House. In recent years the house has been restored and furnished with Victorian originals. A visit guided by knowledgeable and enthusiastic volunteers gives a glimpse into the life of well-to-do Americans during the period.

We tend to think of the Victorians as being sedate, subdued and refined, in part because the black and white photographs, which are the most accessible record of the period, have washed colours from our collective memory. But both Shaw's house and the Kresko Victorian garden next to it display a boisterous side. Inside the house, wallpaper is colourful, with a flashy flower motif in the dining room. Outside, the Kresko garden is planted in equally dazzling annuals: in spring the orange, purple and red are so intense that the colours seem to vibrate against each other. The display is in keeping with Victorian taste, though. Plant "tapestries" composed of horticultural wonders recently imported from the far-flung reaches of empire were the vogue for much of the period, as were new varieties bred by plantsmen delighted to be working with exotic stock.

Near the focal point of the floral display stands another of Shaw's sculptural acquisitions—the Classically-inspired "Juno" by nineteenth century Italian sculpture Carolo Nicoli, who also did the copy of the "Victory." The statue is carved from pure white marble, and represents, viewed one way, an ironic tribute to the problems of memory. Just as the Victorians' love of colour has been obscured by time, so was the fact that many statues of antiquity were originally brightly painted. It is only recently that archeological research had turned up paint traces on many of them.

Just south of this brilliant parterre, the visitor passes another witty imitation. The Kaesar Maze summons up memories of the Great Maze at Hampton Court Palace near London. To look down into it, climb the stairs to the nearby Piper Observatory. The wooden structure recreates a tower built by Shaw to overlook a maze in Tower Grove Park. To the left, sits the Shoenberg Administration Building whose northern portion had been Shaw's city house, which was moved to the Garden from downtown St. Louis a few years after his death.

Directly across from the administration building is one of the most beautiful examples of new directions the Garden is taking—the Shoenberg Fountain. Its simple form contrasts starkly with the elaborateness of Victorian Tower Grove House and the administration building. The fountain consists of an inclined right triangle made from a slab of stone a meter and a half (about five feet) on a side. A triangular viewing court marked on the ground faces it, matching hypotenuse to hypotenuse. Water flows from the upper edges of the raised triangle, introducing enough turbulence to form standing waves that descend the stone slab like a moving design, a fascinating effect that the visitor can watch while sitting on nearby benches.

Shoenberg Fountain, 1975.
Courtesy Missouri Botanical Garden.

The trees to the west, which shade the area so pleasantly, are *Metasequoias* or dawn redwoods planted in 1948, just a few years after the parent trees were found in China. Until then, the species was known only from fossils and was thought to have gone extinct millions of years ago. Once living specimens were discovered, botanists wasted no time in distributing seeds of this ancestor of California's sequoia trees around the world. Today nearly every botanical garden worth its salt has one or more of these proud trees. The Missouri garden's trees are large and interestingly gnarled.

To the left are the shady paths of the English Woodland Garden. To recreate this ecosystem in St. Louis was a challenge since average temperatures range from a Singapore-like 26 degrees Celsius (78 F) in July and August to 2 degrees C (35 F) in the December, January and February.

The Ruth Palmer Blanke Boxwood garden a little further to the west also presented a challenge. There are no native North American boxwoods, and those transplanted from European settings are notoriously difficult to grow in the Midwest. But the late Edgar Anderson, former director of the garden and a boxwood admirer, set up a program to find hardy strains from the Balkans and Asia. Some of these have been used in a formal parterre, while others are planted as specimens accompanied by explanatory material. The boxwood garden is set in a walled area with boxwood planted to form Henry Shaw's initials. At the far end, three fountains send water leaping into the air, the jets timed so that they seem to defy gravity.

CHINESE AND JAPANESE GARDENS

North of the boxwood garden lies the Margaret Grigg Nanjing Friendship Garden, a small "scholar's garden" done in the style of China's southern provinces. This is an intimate area designed for reflection where the scent of jasmine on a late spring afternoon is enough to inspire poetry. Walls enclose the garden on two sides and the visitor enters through a traditional circular moon gate. Inside are a pavilion which was fabricated in St. Louis's sister city Nanjing, as well as a stream, pond, and carefully chosen plantings which carry symbolic meaning and demonstrate the diversity and importance of China's native plants. There are some 30,000 species of plants in China, twice as many as in the continental United States. Many familiar ornamentals like azaleas, rhododendrons, camellias, gardenias, hibiscus, peonies, chrysanthemums, and gingkos are Chinese natives introduced within the last 300 years to the rest of the world. But this little garden is only a small part of the Missouri Botanical Garden's involvement in China. The Garden is also jointly publishing an English language version of the fifty-volume *Flora of China* with Science Press of Beijing.

The 5.6 hectare (fourteen acre) Japanese garden at the southern edge of the botanical garden presents an even more profound exposure to the traditions of another culture. It is a world in microcosm, featuring carefully designed replicas of natural waterfalls and mountain gorges as well as beaches and islands set in a lovely and large irregularly-shaped lake. Each feature is laden with symbolism and invites contemplation from several viewpoints.

The Japanese garden's plantings does not rely on flowers—although iris and chrysanthemums are found in it—but on subtly varying shades of foliage to make its effects. Stone lanterns and small bamboo and stone fountains are placed throughout the garden. During warm weather the constant presence of water refreshes both body and spirit, while after winter storms many of the lanterns display snow as if it were flowers. As in the Chinese garden, contemplation of the Japanese garden brings both spiritual rewards and the pleasure of a rich and different way of viewing nature.

At the time that Henry Shaw was making his plan for a botanical garden a reality, none of the Japanese plants and few of the Chinese ones were known to the Western world. Japan had been effectively closed to the West for 250 years, except for the Dutch outpost on Deshima Island. Intrepid plant collectors outfitted by the Jardin des Plantes in Paris and by Kew had been collecting in China for some time, but the vastness of the country insured that China's secrets would be revealed only over several decades.

Spreading the word about the new discoveries from all over the world, and finding the ones which might be useful in the Midwest, were high on Shaw's list of priorities. He set aside a large area for new fruit and hardwood trees, for example. He would find today's William Kemper Center for Home Gardening a very good idea.

Here the home gardener will find hundreds of suggestions—from what vegetables are suitable for the St. Louis area, through to which plants attract butterflies—displayed in twenty-three small demonstration gardens spread over 3.3 hectares (8.3 acres.) The Kemper Center building itself is home to master gardeners trained to answer home gardeners' questions. They respond to more than 25,000 calls a year.

The Kemper Center also has several colonies of bees, but unlike the hives at Leiden, you can safely look inside these. The bees enter through a small, inconspicuous opening on the side of the Kemper Center, and from inside the building you can see through the glass backs of the hives and watch the bees busily depositing their nectar and building their honey combs.

Near the beds of flowers outside in the Kemper Center courtyard or underneath the nearby fruit trees when they are in bloom, the visitor can experience what attracts bees to flowers—their frangrance. The perfumes entice bees inside the flowers where they pick up pollen or nutritive nectar from the male parts to carry back to the hive. In the process pollen is transferred to the female parts of flowers, which is essential for the plant to produce seeds. Butterflies, moths, dragonflies and birds are also attracted to fragrant flowers. So are the beetles which Ghillean Prance found pollinating the huge waterlily *Victoria amazonica*. According to a brochure for visitors to the Kemper Center, in the United States fifteen percent of all food and textile crops depend on insect pollination. It adds that insecticides threaten the honey bee population. Integrated pest management, which aims at cutting down on insecticides by substituting biological and other methods to get rid of pests, is promoted by the Kemper Center counselors.

The complex of buildings to the north and east of the Kemper Center is where that message and its many corollaries are elaborated, and where Missouri Botanical Garden's reaches the most people with the word about the importance of biodiversity.

Climatron and Biodiversity

The Climatron is the central building in the complex. Its design is based on R. Buckminster Fuller's principles, relying on a complex network of triangles to form the framework for a spherical, domed surface. The structure needs no extra interior support. At the centre it rises to twenty-one meters (seventy feet), and at its base it measures 52.5 meters (175 feet) in diameter. When it was opened in 1960 as a greenhouse for tropical plants, it was the only geodesic dome used as a greenhouse and was hailed as a significant architectural achievement.

Since then the dome has been refurbished and linked to two adjacent structures, the Shoenberg Temperate House and the Brookings Interpretative Center. Together they combine recreations of tropical and temperate climates with interactive displays to convey the Garden's message.

The Temperate House has a southward-sloping roof to catch the sun's rays, while a computerized climate control system maintains the temperature between 4 and 32 degrees C (40 and 90 degrees F.) The plants grown here originate from many geographic regions—chiefly California, Chile, the Mediterranean basin, South Africa and Australian coastal regions. All require protection during St. Louis's winters, and some would find life outside during the city's summers far too hot and rainy.

The temperature in the Climatron, on the other hand, ranges between 18 to 24 degrees C (64 to 75 degrees F), with average relative humidity of 85 percent. Walk up its gradually ascending ramps, and you pass through several layers of rain forest. Bananas, cacao, coffee and coconuts are among the 1,100 different species growing here. In an exhibit about food from the tropics, you can eat samples from some of the food plants. The dome is also home to free-flying birds and butterflies, while pools and acquariums shelter tropical fish.

The path through the Climatron takes you to the entrance of the Brooking Interpretive Center where more teaching exhibits are found. Life-size figures of an ecologist, a forest dweller, a land developer, and a farmer greet you in a diorama presenting different viewpoints on the question of deforestation. Other exhibits display a running total of human population growth and species extinction as well as photos of different environments such as grassland, rain forests, and deciduous forests.

The importance of maintaining the earth's biodiversity rings through all the multimedia presentations. The inside spread of the Garden's welcoming brochure also trumpets: "Plants are essential to life on earth. The quality of human life, our very survival, depends on the health of our global environment. Everything we do affects the environment, and we are all responsible for protecting it."

Yet, while mention is made of threats to the environment in the developed world, the emphasis is on what is happening in the tropics. Much of the Garden's work which the visitor does not see is directed toward the region. In fact, the Missouri Botanical Garden is currently doing more for the cataloguing and study of tropical flora on the Malay peninsula than the Singapore Botanical Garden can, in large part because the Missouri garden's resources are so much larger. It has taken its research role extremely seriously for more than one hundred years.

Furthermore, unlike researchers for many other large institutions who only spend short periods of time in the areas they are studying, scientists from Missouri frequently sign on to spend years in the field. Staff from the garden have moved to Madagascar, Bolivia, Venezuela, and elsewhere to work in close collaboration with local scientists and institutions. Director Peter Raven explains that the Garden believes it is important to share expertise with scientists in the wider world both by welcoming graduate students to the garden and by working with local research institutions for extended periods.

Ten percent of the world has eighty percent of the world's scientific and engineering experts. Of the remaining twenty percent, forty percent of the experts are found in China, Brazil, Mexico, and India. Where much botanical work should be going on trained scientists and engineers are thin on the ground. According to Raven, the Missouri Garden has an obligation to help out.

RESEARCH AROUND THE WORLD

Two major Garden projects contain much information about the wealth of plants found in the tropics. The *Flora Mesoamerica* will catalogue the plants of Southern Mexico and Central America. The *Flora of the Venezuelan Highlands* is a two-volume work on the "Lost World" of the highlands of Venezuela, where nearly inaccessible tabletop mountains are home to some 10,000 species of plants, many of which are found nowhere else in the world.

One of the Garden's priorities for the next decade is to do more of this sort of research, to conduct intensive, long-term inventories of selected sites in South America. The data will be used to develop a plant inventory of the Western Hemisphere. A Center for Conservation and Sustainable Development will also be launched to explore and implement new approaches to the conservation and sustainable use of plant diversity.

Research has always been one of the Missouri Botanical Garden's strengths. Shaw's scientific advisors, including Kew's Sir William Hooker, persuaded him to establish close links with Washington University of St. Louis. He provided a yearly stipend for a botany school to be known as the Henry Shaw School of Botany, and endowed a chair which was named in honour of George Engelmann. Currently the head of the botany school is, ex officio, the second-in-command at the botanical garden, and about half of the Garden's $23 million budget goes toward research.

One of the principal ways the Garden's research is disseminated is through TROPICOS, the Internet version of the Garden's database which was started in the 1980s when computer technology was in its infancy. Now researchers have access to nearly 1.5 million specimen records on-line, many including photographs or botanical drawings as well as descriptions and information about distribution and physiology. The database is said to be the most comprehensive and widely used in the world; it receives more than 7,000 requests for information a day.

The Monsanto Center, the Garden's flagship research facility on Shaw Boulevard a short walk from the Garden, opened in 1998 in an area which had once been light industrial but which was deteriorating. The building of a research facility here and not in a suburb has been hailed as a sign of the Garden's commitment to the revitalization of the neighbourhood. The building certainly is impressive. With seven storeys, it is higher than anything in the immediate surroundings, and the upper floors offer views as far as Gateway Arch on the Mississippi. To gain access, you must be cleared by a guard who sits alone on the first floor which is paneled in woods from around the world. The facility has laboratories, a library, and herbarium facilities which are protected by the latest in climate and humidity control. It is evident that major money went into building it.

But how can a garden which purports to be so dedicated to the preservation of the world's biodiversity be so heavily indebted to Monsanto, one of the world's largest chemical companies whose specialties include pesticides, herbicides, and genetically modified plants? Aren't Monsanto products among the biggest sinners? Raven points out that Monsanto was founded in St. Louis in 1905 and has supported all major cultural and charitable activities in the city ever since. It is only normal, he says, that Monsanto has contributed to the garden since its beginnings, just as many other local St. Louis firms have. He sees the big problem as agriculture itself. Monoculture, the exclusive cultivation of one sort of crop has existed since the 1930s when hybrid corn replaced all other corn varieties in the U.S. Midwest.

MAKING AGRICULTURE PRODUCTIVE

"Humans have been farming for more than 10,000 years, and agriculture has driven back biodiversity where ever you look," he explains. But "the more productive agricultural land can be, the less impact there will be on more marginal land, and marginal land like the jungles of the tropics or dry, currently uncultivated grasslands are those most threatened today. We lose about one-third of our crops to pests like insects and weeds. If genetically modified plants can cut that down, it will be all to the good. "

That kind of argument is not very popular in some quarters. Raven has even had invitations to speak revoked when the sponsoring organization learned of his views on genetic modification. But it is hard to doubt either Raven's sincerity or his credentials. He's been the Missouri Botanical Garden's director since 1971, when he was a thirty-five-year-old botanist who had just done some ground-breaking work at Stanford University with fellow biologist Paul Ehrlich. They proposed that plants and animals evolve together in a sort of chemical arms race. Plant species which develop chemicals that make them inedible are going to do better than plants which don't, they argued. However if the animal species which usually eat the plants chances on a way to detoxify the plants' chemical weapons, the plant species is going to suffer until, by another random genetic mutation, the plant develops new toxins. The result of this see-saw are animals that depend on particular kinds of plants. That means that endangering a plant species often endangers an animal species too.

A corollary to this process is seen where plants and animals evolve together in a mutually beneficial way. The beetle which feeds inside that famous waterlily *Victoria amazonica* is an example. The lily provides food for the beetle which carries pollen away with it to pollinate other flowers. Raven and Ehrlich called this coevolution, and the concept has become an important one as scientists strive to understand the natural world. Their original articles are cited again and again in the literature about biodiversity and ecology, as well as that of evolutionary research.

But Raven is not only an original scientific thinker, he is a man of great energy and considerable administrative skills. When he took over the director's job, the Missouri Botanical Garden was beginning to struggle out of thirty years of doldrums. Budgets had been balanced by the previous director and a new herbarium and library building started, but the Garden was a merely a garden with a regional reputation in a city whose Golden Age seemed long past.

That has changed. The Missouri Botanical Garden can now rightly compare itself to Kew and the New York Botanical Garden in terms of its research activities. Its public education and outreach programs are among

The famous waterlily, *Victoria amazonica*, at the Missouri Botanical Garden in Victorian times. The Linnaeus House is in the background.
Courtesy of Missouri Botanical Garden.

the best anywhere, and the gardens themselves are gorgeous. Raven has been singularly successful in taking to the world his vision of what the role of botanical gardens should be.

"Today people are less and less in touch with nature, and with the places and ways in which their food is produced," he says. "Fifty percent of the world's population lives in urban areas, and soon that proportion will rise to eighty percent. Botanical gardens in the future will become even more important as places for contact with the natural world."

He says that in the more than three decades that he's been involved with botanical gardens, he has learned that people want to "appreciate, celebrate, and safeguard" nature. The appreciating and celebrating are the easy parts of the equation. To do what is necessary to safeguard nature is much more difficult.

Raven recently told *World Book* that "avoiding the destruction of so many of the other organisms... is the right thing to do from a moral, ethical, or religious point of view. As far as we know, the living things that share the world with us are the only living things in the whole universe. That alone ought to give us a respect or reverence for life. It ought to make us want to avoid driving the species into extinction permanently."

THE CHALLENGE AHEAD

And while much of this species destruction is occurring in poor, under-developed, tropical countries, in many respects those countries are only pawns in the global game, Raven says. "The planet is at the mercy of the industrialized nations which account for only twenty-three per cent of the world's population, but use about ninety percent of the resources that support life on Earth."

Reducing the resources that rich nations use through energy conservation, recycling, and reduced consumption is important. So may be forgiving the foreign debt of the poor countries if they agree to set aside protected habitats in national parks, although some nations are too poor to do even that, Raven notes. "...Anything that would stop or even slow down the flow of money from poor nations to rich ones would help solve many of humanity's problems... Eliminating poverty would give us a chance to nurture more of the human talent in the world for solving our other problems."

The private sector and volunteers have a role to play in this, but

The Clusius Garden at the Hortus Botanicus – a taste of what a
botanical garden was like more than 400 years ago.

The beautiful blooms of the South African plant *clivia* can be found
in the greenhouses of the Hortus Botanicus.

The long parterres east of the Grand Galerie at the Jardin des Plantes
in Paris are full of tulips in May.

Irises grace the Jardin des Plantes in spring.

Augusta, Princess of Wales, had the Chinese pagoda constructed in
the mid-seventeenth century. It is now a Kew landmark.

Bluebells make a May Day spectacle in the Conservation Area near
Queen Charlotte's Cottage in the Royal Botanical Gardens at Kew.

Kew's Victorian garden designers reveled in bright colours like this display of tulips.

Heliconia blooms near the Singapore Botanic Gardens' Visitor Centre.

The cannonball tree (*Couroupita guianensis*) has one of the largest seeds in the world. Several specimen trees grace the Singapore Botanic Gardens.

Water lilies in Singapore's Sundial Garden.

Henry Shaw, founder of the Missouri Botanical Garden,
lies buried behind this gate reminiscent of Decimus Burton's gates at Kew.

Henry Shaw fell in love with the prairie near St. Louis where
the Missouri Botanical Garden is today.

The hemlock forest at the heart of the New York Botanical Garden is a remnant of the forest which once covered the region.

The demonstration gardens at the New York Botanical Garden offer beauty
and peace as well as gardening ideas for visitors.

The Jardin botanique de Montréal's Chinese Garden,
inspired by private gardens of the Ming Dynasty (1368-1644),
is intriguing in all seasons.

Butterflies love the late summer flowers at the Jardin botanique de Montréal.

Goldenrod stands out against the waterfall at Montreal's Alpine Garden, much like the burning torch that was supposed to guard the entrance to Eden.

The Primitive Plant Garden at the Strybing Arboretum and Botanical Garden brings together living relatives of plant groups that once dominated the earth.

Frederick Law Olmsted never thought it was possible sand dunes would be transformed into this beautiful San Francisco parkland.

Strybing's magnolia collection is one of the finest in the world.

Clematis at the University of British Columbia Botanical Garden.

The British Columbia Native Plant Garden.
From its beginning the University of British Columbia Botanical Garden
has catalogued and promoted plants native to the region.

ultimately many of the commitments are going to have to come from governments. "Realistically, the most efficient way to provide large amounts of money for any purpose is for people to voluntarily tax themselves," he told *World Book*. "When you're talking about major social problems, we can never deliver more than a small amount of what's needed through volunteerism or private industry. Those things can make important contributions, but only government intervention can deliver the goods."

Tough words, but then the problems Raven is addressing are tough. Given their magnitude, it is hard not to be discouraged. But, of course, when you're discouraged is one of the best times to visit any botanical garden, and perhaps particularly the Missouri Botanical Garden. The visitor might do well to take another quick look around the Garden before leaving its carefully managed beauty.

In the middle of the open area south of the Linnaeus House and west of the Climatron, lies the Dry Streambed Garden which, significantly perhaps, does not have a corporate sponsor. In it rare and endangered North American species which can grow in St. Louis' climate are planted. The little garden provides a glimpse of what we might be losing, and what we can save.

Prairie wildflowers.
Photo by Mary Soderstrom.

Enid A. Haupt Conservatory.
Photo by Mary Soderstrom.

Toward an American Kew...and Beyond

THE NEW YORK BOTANICAL GARDEN got started forty years after the botanical gardens in Singapore and St. Louis, but it is just as deeply rooted in the nineteenth century English botanical tradition as they are. In fact, so the story goes, the idea of the garden goes back to 1888 when intrepid American botanist and philanthropist Nathaniel Lord Britton and his wife Elizabeth took a belated honeymoon trip to England.

"Oh, why can't we have a garden just like that!" she exclaimed after one day spent at the Royal Gardens at Kew, her husband said later. Most likely she was not the first young wife to be swept away by Kew's wonders, but she and her husband were among the few people who could actually hope to create an American Kew.

The pair were botany-loving offspring of well-connected New York families. Britton, born to a family of Staten Island landowners, was teaching geology and botany at Columbia, and would later receive his Ph.D. after writing a thesis on the flora of New Jersey. Elizabeth Knight Britton had graduated at seventeen from what is now New York's Hunter College, and had gone on to develop a deep interest in mosses. It was she who put forward the idea of making a botanical garden at a meeting of the Torrey Botanical Club in October 1888. The club, which counted several wealthy and intellectual New Yorkers among its members, successfully campaigned to use part of the 1,500 hectares (about 3,750 acres) of open land that had been put aside a few years earlier for parks in the northern part of the city.

This wasn't the first attempt to set up a botanical garden in New York. In 1801 Dr. David Hosack, who had trained in medicine in Edinburgh and London, bought twenty acres in central Manhattan with the idea of developing both a medicinal garden and one open to the public interested in botany. A professor at Columbia, he built his own greenhouse for tender plants, and grew flowers and vegetables as well on the land which was at that time three miles from the center of the city. Two of his students went on to become among the nineteenth century's most prominent botanists— Asa Gray, who among other things advised Henry Shaw in the development of the Missouri Botanical Garden, and John Torrey, after whom the botany club to which the Brittons belonged was named.

But running your own botanical garden is an expensive proposition.

Elizabeth Britton, botanist and co-founder of the
New York Botanical Garden.
Archives of the LuEsther T. Mertz Library, NYBG.

By 1810 the costs were up to $100,000 a year, far beyond what Dr. Hosack could afford. That year he sold the land to the state of New York for $4,807.36. Four years later the state transferred the property to Columbia which was still in the throes of getting established. Without the resources to operate the garden, Columbia eventually leased out most of the land. Wisely, however, it held onto the title, because in time the land became extremely valuable. In 1928 the university sold 200 parcels covering about three city blocks to John D. Rockefeller for $100 million to build Rockefeller Center. Even before the sale, income from the land helped build Columbia into a first-class university.

Another serious, and much less financially successful, attempt to create a botanical garden was undertaken in 1877. The idea was to sell $25 shares to finance a public display garden at the edge of Central Park. The plan needed 14,000 shares to be sold, but the goal was not reached.

When the Brittons became involved, though, the stars were right for a botanical garden. In 1891 the state legislature approved the use of 100 hectares (250 acres) in Bronx Park for the botanical garden. The city of New York then agreed to put up $500,000 for buildings and landscaping, provided that $250,000 in private funds be raised.

This is where good connections came in handy. Andrew Carnegie, Cornelius Vanderbilt, and J. Pierpont Morgan, three of the richest and most powerful men in the country at the time, had been persuaded to become officers of the botanic garden corporation. They each put up $25,000, convinced friends like John D. Rockefeller and the Hon. Addison Brown to give similar amounts, and collected the balance from businesses like Tiffany & Company. In so doing they started the new garden off on a sound financial basis, and also set a precedent for involvement by New York's financial and intellectual elite.

The New York Botanical Garden is well past its hundredth birthday now and private support plays an even bigger role. Governmental agencies provided close to two-thirds of the funds to build the garden initially; in 2000, government sources provided only twenty-one percent of operating revenues. This shift says some profound things about society's priorities which the visitor might ponder during a leisurely visit to the garden.

The NYBG was opened well before the automobile age with the idea that in addition to scientific research, the garden would be "a place of agreeable resort for the public at large." The section of Bronx Park chosen for the garden is conveniently near the New York Central railway line, and the main entrance was built just across from the station. (The NYBG was following Kew's excellent example; by 1900 more than a million garden lovers at year were getting off at Kew Bridge Station and Kew Gardens Station on their way to a day's outing in the Royal Garden.) Today you can still enter there but the main entrance has been switched to the west side of the Garden where flatter terrain allows for parking lots.

THE GREEN ROUTE TO THE NYBG

Driving in New York City presents all the problems that driving in any big city does, and then some, but with a little planning a visitor can follow a scenic, and mostly green route to reach the Garden. From Manhattan, travel north on the Henry Hudson Parkway, which passes through some of the oldest woods in the metropolitan area at the northern tip of the island. Then cut over toward the Mosholu Parkway, pass underneath the Major Deegan Expressway, and follow the signs to the NYBG.

There is a certain appropriateness about taking this route. Henry Hudson was an English captain sailing in Dutch service and searching for a Northwest Passage to the Far East when he explored the Hudson River in 1609 (the year of the death of Clusius, the father of the Hortus Botanicus at Leiden). It also was the year of the first voyages of the Dutch East Indies Company, which was to loom so large in the history of European exploration of the world and in the world's flora.

At the Garden's entrance, visitors receive brochures which contain several suggestions on how to organize a visit, depending on the season, since the NYBG is too big and too varied to see in one day. With forty-eight different garden areas and collections it lives up to its nickname, the Garden of Gardens. A good way to get your bearings in any season is to take a tram ride as an introduction. It goes up hill and down dale, and lets passengers off at three stops where they can look around and then catch another tram.

A walking tour can start with a turn to the left at the main entrance, into the area which was the center of the Garden's recent multi-year revitalization plan. One of the first collections is the Conifer Arboretum which features a wide variety of evergreen conifers and is a particular pleasure to see covered with snow in winter. Nearby is the herb garden. In summer it displays 150 species of herbs used in medicine or cooking, all planted within boxwood hedges like those found in Europe's early medicinal gardens. The visitor might be tempted to sit down on one of the benches and enjoy the fragrance wafting from the plants, but it is also easy to be lured onward into the perennial garden next door. Here hosta lilies, Japanese anemones, phlox, and other shade-loving plants in cool colors of blue, pink, white and gray are planted under century-old pine trees. Beside them in the garden's sunny section grow sun-loving plants like red-hot pokers in red, orange, and yellow.

Building the Palm House Conservatory, November 1899.
From the archives of The LuEsther T. Mertz Library, NYBG.

The Conservatory, 1916.
From the archives of The LuEsther T. Mertz Library, NYBG.

Just beyond these gardens and to the left, is the Enid A. Haupt Conservatory, one of the great symbols of the New York Botanical Garden. It faces
northwest toward the Garden's lawns and its other landmark edifice, the
old Museum building. Until recently the Museum housed the Herbarium
and the LuEsther T. Mertz Library, which have just moved to a brand new
facility nearby, the International Plant Science Center. Now that the space
has been freed, the original building will be restored to its former splendor.

The Enid A. Haupt Conservatory

The Conservatory, a few years younger than the Museum, is a Victorian
glass house inspired by the Palm House at Kew. Many say it surpasses the
building which inspired it because of its elegant proportions and the way
it wraps around the water gardens set behind it. When it opened in June
1900, thousands of people lined up to see inside. There were 9,000 plants,
most of them transferred from Columbia University where they had been
stored, waiting for a permanent home. Others were gifts including five
palm trees which had grown so tall they were pushing at the roof of a
private conservatory, a ten-foot (2.5 meter) high rubber tree plant, orchids
from the Far East, and tree ferns. So many plants were either donated or
already in the collection that Nathaniel Lord Britton only had to spend
$100 of the $10,000 allotted to fill the greenhouse.

The plants inside the Conservatory prospered and the great glass house
attracted tens of thousands of visitors over the following decades. While
most were charmed by the chance to visit something so exotic, others felt
more at home. One such visitor was a lion who escaped from the Bronx
Zoo in 1916 and wandered over to inspect the grounds of the Gardens.
Zoo and Garden employees as well as civil authorities spent several anxious
hours combing the Garden for the beast. But, no fool, the lion had made
his way into the Conservatory and when found was curled up, asleep, in
the notch of a tree beneath the conservatory's central dome.

Tropical plant houses may be beautiful and inviting, but they also are
difficult to maintain since the year-round humidity essential to the plants
also rusts iron framework and rots wood. The conservatory was refurbished
in 1935, 1952, and again in 1975 when it appeared that it would have to
undergo major renovations or be torn down. The timing could not have
been worse because New York City was in the midst of a fiscal crisis, and
bankruptcy was a distinct possibility. With little governmental support in

prospect, the Garden's board turned to private donors. The effort sputtered along for a while until Enid Annenberg Haupt stepped in. A member of the Garden's board, heiress to a publishing fortune and former publisher and editor of *Seventeen* magazine, Mrs. Haupt agreed to provide $5 million for restoration work, and another $5 million as a fund for maintenance.

Twenty years later, the conservatory was again in need of major repairs, this time to the tune of $25 million. Mrs. Haupt helped out handsomely once more as did other philanthropists and various levels of government. This latest restoration took four years and uncovered some unexpected problems, such as twenty layers of lead-based paint which took months to remove. When the conservatory reopened its doors in 1997, it had not only state-of-the-art heating and ventilation systems, but also all of the gorgeous filigree and detail work which had made the original construction so beautiful, had been restored.

The visitor should allow an hour or more to wander through A World of Plants, as the exhibits inside are called. You can travel from orchid-festooned jungle trees to Old and New World deserts without getting jet-lagged or tired. The basic message of the conservatory—as of the entire Garden—is set forward in the conservatory's guidebook:

> Without green plants it is unlikely that there would be any other life on earth, without them and without the remarkable process of photosynthesis, which no scientist has been able to replicate in the laboratory, where would we get the oxygen in the air? Where would we obtain the foods that sustain us; the fuels that warm us; the roofs that shelter us; the wines for celebrating; or the medicines for treating pain and diseases today and in the future?

Seasonal Flowers and Demonstration Gardens

And where else would we find such beauty? On the northeast side of the conservatory is the peony collection, where fifty-eight different herbaceous peonies bloom from early to mid-May. A little earlier in the year, the nearby Seasonal Walk which runs in front of the conservatory flamboyantly displays more than 13,000 tulip bulbs, which are later replaced by plantings of annual flowers, from zinnias to giant cannas. Near the end of the Walk is a series of small, intimate gardens. Cut flowers, vegetables, compost, shade, fragrance: each demonstration garden specializes in something specific. This area was converted from lawn in 1989 and in ten years the shrubs, trees, and perennials in the demonstration gardens tripled in size. That means that stepping inside the thicket at the middle of one of them, the Della J. Bryce Wildlife Garden, is to lose yourself as surely as if you were in the middle of a forest with a thick under-storey. The little garden contains a wide variety of plants that appeal to many sorts of animals, including the *Buddleia davidii*, or butterfly bush, which attracts Monarch butterflies. This kind of plant was sent back to France from China by Father Armand David, and is featured in another small garden in the Jardin des Plantes in Paris.

The wildlife garden could inspire you to create a mini-forest back home. A real forest, however, is the heart of the New York Botanical Garden— literally and figuratively. At the Garden's center lies 16 hectares (40 acres) of first growth, mixed hardwood forest. Most of what is now the city of New York was covered with similar forest when the Dutch first arrived. This remnant is a unique reminder of what the landscape was like before Europeans wrested control from the indigenous population.

HEMLOCK FOREST

Hemlock, the tree eulogized by Longfellow in his poem about the noble Indian warrior Hiawatha, was the most common tree on the low hills around what is now the Bronx. The NYBG forest has been protected for more than a hundred years, but the balance within it is changing. Part of that change is due to natural processes. As trees mature, the forest canopy becomes thicker and sun-loving plants cannot survive on the forest floor so the balance shifts among the kinds of trees taking root.

Part of the change, however, is directly due to what humans have been doing around the forest. During the summers at the turn of the twentieth century when as many as 50,000 people visited on a Sunday, residents of tenements of the Lower East Side were known to camp out in the forest. Some sixty years later, ROTC cadets from nearby Fordham University bivouacked among the trees.

Worse damage, though, has been done indirectly by humans. Hemlock woolly adelgids are little insects not native to North America. They arrived in imported hemlock timber and spread throughout the Northeast on the wind, on birds' feet, and in the fur of animals. They are munching away at the NYBG forest's hemlocks right now, weakening some trees so that they are easier for high winds to blow down, and killing others outright.

American beeches, oaks, and tulip trees are taking the hemlocks' place, joined by some trees that are far from their home territory. Among them is the Asian Amur corktree, a native of the Amur river basin in the vast forest area between Russian and China. Those with a taste for irony may smile at the fact that the only relics of Amerindian culture in the Bronx are a few petroglyphs, while the hemlock forest is being invaded by trees whose origins lie not far from where the Amerindian migration to North America appears to have begun.

The paths into the forest are inviting, and you can take a self-guided tour. Or you can get a good look into it, by taking the path along the Bronx River which passes by an old snuff factory.

The Bronx River is the only freshwater river in New York City since the Hudson and the East rivers at this point are really saltwater estuaries. Compared to them, the Bronx looks puny, yet since the end of the last Ice Age it has gouged out a canyon along a fault line in the underlying rock. It also watered farmland in the rolling country north of the Garden and, in the Garden, powered a mill to make snuff from tobacco. The P. Lorillard family grew tobacco for decades on their 661-acre estate before it was bought for Bronx Park. It is to them that we owe the fact that the Garden's precious forest was not cut down.

In many ways, the Garden's forest symbolizes the work that the NYBG is doing in the forests around the world. It is bad enough that more than ninety percent of the original forests in the contiguous United States have been cut down, while final stands of virgin timber are being logged intensively now in Canada and Alaska.

But, while many species of plants were displaced or made extinct as Europeans pushed their way inland, botanists and plant explorers examined most of North America between the beginning of the seventeenth and the middle of the nineteenth century. They sent samples of plants, seeds and cuttings to European botanical gardens. Some of the transported species are now actually more widely distributed than they were originally. The black locust, for example, is native to a relatively small area in the southern Appalachians, but now grows wild all over Europe (where only one stand of virgin forest remains, in Poland.)

With tropical forests, it is a different story. We are nowhere near close to cataloguing all the plants that are out there, but we do know that there are some very useful ones among those which have been studied. An example is the rosy periwinkle, *Catharanthus roseus*, which has become the poster-child for the movement to safeguard the earth's biodiversity. After this pretty little native of Madagascar was introduced to Europe, in 1757 at the Jardin des Plantes, it spread around the world. It was and is planted widely in flower gardens, where it is sometimes known as Madagascar periwinkle, or *Vinca rosea*, but the plant also has been used as an herbal remedy for sore throat, pleurisy, dysentery, and diabetes. When Western scientists experimented with it in the 1950s, hoping for a new diabetes treatment, to their surprise they discovered periwinkle contains compounds useful in the treatment of childhood leukemia and Hodgkin's disease. Since 1957 the death rate from childhood leukemia has dropped from 84 percent to five percent, largely because of drugs with a periwinkle base. The plant, which by itself is toxic, contains more than seventy alkaloids with medical applications such as lowering blood sugar levels, reducing bleeding, and tranquilizing.

The rosy periwinkle story raises an important question: how many other plants now growing in tropical regions could be useful in modern medicine? Some 1,300 plants are used by natives of the Amazon basin for medical purposes, while another 6,500 plants are used in Asian herbal medicine. Very few of these, however, have been studied by scientists. The great fear of many is that plants as valuable as the rosy periwinkle will disappear without ever being studied properly.

"Today we are witnessing the greatest mass extinction since a giant meteorite crashed into our planet, eliminating the dinosaurs and other less charismatic life forms," says Brian M. Boom, NYBG's vice president for Botanical Science and Pfizer Curator of Botany. At the rate that we are destroying habitats and burning forests, the 300,000 species of plants which exist today on our planet maybe reduced by a third by 2050.

How to improve this situation? According to Boom:

We depend primarily on governments, private landowners, and environmental advocacy groups to save biodiversity by setting aside land as protected areas, and on industry to devise ways to use bio-diversity by developing new foods, fibers, fuels and medicines. But institutions such as the NYBG must conduct the basic research that is done nowhere else.

RESEARCH DISCOVERS NEW SPECIES

Currently the NYBG has 150 ongoing research projects in twenty countries, involving more than 160 scientists and graduate students. This research is nothing new: Ghillean Prance—now Sir Ghillean, director of Kew for eleven years and involved in the Eden Project—started his career with a post doctoral fellowship on an NYBG project in the Amazon basin in the early 1960s. Currently the NYBG operates an international graduate studies program in partnership with five universities: Yale, New York, Columbia, CCNY and Cornell. The master plan for the first seven years of the twenty-first century calls for the NYBG to become "the world's premier institution for the discovery and interpretation of plant diversity and the complex inter-relationships between plants and people."

In recent years that research has discovered a new species in the mango family from Amazonia, a new species of moss from Costa Rica, two new species in the frankincense family from French Guyana, a new species in the coffee family from Ecuador, two new species of the citrus family from South America, and many others.

The Garden is home to hundreds of varieties of plants which are endangered or extinct in the wild. In all, 18,000 scientific groups of plants and 40,000 individual plants are represented in the living collections, while the herbarium has 6,500,000 specimens.

This intimidating bunch of statistics should not interfere with enjoying the Garden. It is, after all, a place for ordinary folk to enjoy themselves. Increasing the audience for the Garden, in fact, was a major preoccupation at the end of the twentieth century; the long hard fight to safeguard the earth's green richness is lost before it is begun if society in the broadest sense is not enlisted.

GARDENS FOR CHILDREN

To get a good idea of one way the Garden proposes to do this, turn right at the Main Entrance when you enter. This route leads toward the Everett Children's Adventure Garden. The idea for this garden designed specifically for children dates back to the early 1990s, when the NYBG undertook some serious thinking about its future. At that time it was attracting around 400,000 visitors a year and really could not consider attracting many more given the facilities in place at that time. A weekend crowd of 20,000, who came to see the magnolias and azaleas at the height of their beauty, could turn into an embarrassment because there weren't enough parking spaces or bathrooms to accommodate the crowds. It was then that a seven year plan to revitalize the garden was undertaken. The goal was to raise $200 million in order to restore the Enid A. Haupt Conservatory, rearrange the parking lots, add bathrooms, and set up a new, hands-on center for kids. The campaign was a grand success: $8 million more than the goal was raised, and already the plan has borne fruit in terms of opening the NYBG to a larger public. By the end of 1999, annual attendance had increased by 50 percent to 600,000 a year, and the goal of one million seemed attainable.

Inside the 12-acre (4.8 hectare) children's adventure site, there is a lot to keep kids busy, even those whose attention span is short and who ordinarily prefer computer and video games. Some of activities are designed for sheer exuberance: three mazes—featuring boulders, meadow grass, and low boxwood hedges—invite running around and games of hide and seek. The garden designers decided to put these at the entrance in order to give kids a chance to let off steam in a new setting and also to prepare them for other sorts of discovery.

The other "rooms" in the long narrow site contain elements geared to the curriculum in New York schools. For example, the exhibit on the parts of plants fits in with first and second grade lesson plans, while the one on pollination complements what is taught third and fourth grades. Other features offer a chance for curious kids to find out what different kinds of dirt are made of or what sorts of muck water birds slurp up from pond bottoms. There also is space for more structured presentations for school groups and where trained teenage volunteers explain about such things as ecosystems on weekends and during the summer.

The idea behind nearly every element in the center is that children should have fun while learning, or rather, that they learn best when having fun. The scale is also kid-size, which may be a little claustrophobic for adults, but this means that a four-year-old can flirt with getting lost in the boxwood maze even though it is no puzzle at all to an adult. On a fine Saturday afternoon the level of activity in the adventure center can be hectic. The exhibits feature bright colours, multi-media displays, giant plastic butterflies, and a huge topiary frog kids squirt by stomping on lily pads. Be forewarned, this not a place for quiet contemplation.

At the far end of the Adventure Center, the visitor can find a sort of antidote. The Center fronts a pond and wetland created a decade ago in a

The Mitsubishi Wild Wetland attracts red-winged blackbirds
and many varieties of water birds.
Photo by Mary Soderstrom.

poorly-drained, swampy section which had been the despair of garden
planners. Instead of fighting the soil conditions, the NYBG decided to encourage them. The result, after some clever work with drainage and water
table, is a natural-appearing wetland, which attracts birds and wildlife.
Take the Mitsubishi Wild Wetland Trail around it for a much quieter nature
experience. Here are benches where you can sit and watch red-winged blackbirds balancing on cattails and hummingbirds feeding on giant mallow flowers,
or check the progress of ducklings as they learn where to find the most
succulent water plants, or simply listen to the wind in the leaves and smell
the spiciness of the wetland plants.

When it is time to move on, the Ruth Rea Howell Family Garden will
give you another take on how to engage children in the botanical world.
The tram stops there, but walkers will find several paths leading in that
direction. (The Olmsted brothers, the sons of Frederick Law Olmsted, who
was the architect of Central Park, laid out a series of roads and paths in the
1920s which is still largely in use today.) In spring the path which leads
past Daffodil Hill and then over to Azalea Way is the one to take. Tens of
thousands of daffodils and narcissus bloom between March and April, while
the azaleas are splendid in May.

Continue along Snuff Mill Road, cross the Bronx River, and continue
past the Peggy Rockefeller Rose Garden where you may be tempted to stop
to admire the grand display of roses. The original roses that grew on the site

were planted by the Lorillards who used them to scent the snuff they made. The current garden was named the Best Public Rose Garden of 1999 by All-America Rose Selection Committee, and contains 2,700 plants of 290 different varieties.

The Family Garden is up the hill, and well worth the effort. The activities for children center around growing things—planting seedlings, harvesting tomatoes, digging around to see how the earth worms are doing. It is a much more low key place than the Adventure Center, and offers experiences which are slower paced. The Children's' Gardening Program is centered here, where the rewards may take a couple of months to arrive in the form of squash or lettuce to take home.

GLOBAL GARDENS

The Ruth Rea Howell Family Garden is also home to the Global Gardens which offer a fascinating glimpse into what plants gardeners grow at home in various places around the world. One recent summer there were gardens with Chinese, Russian, African, and Caribbean flavours. Each was tended by Garden Diplomats, avid gardeners whose roots are in the different geographic areas. The Caribbean garden had passion flower and ginger for example, while the Chinese garden had bitter melon, amaranth, and Chinese celery. Seeds, plants, and guidance are provided by the volunteer gardeners, but what makes the individual gardens special is the love with which they are nurtured. Visitors get a chance to ask questions of the gardeners themselves on weekends from April through October.

While the Family Garden is a good hike from the main entrance, it close to the Waring Pedestrian Entrance which makes it easy for people in the neighbourhood to visit.

The Bronx, of course, was farmland once upon a time. The borough gets its name from Jacob Bronks, a Swedish farmer who settled there in 1639 when the Dutch were beginning colonization. Even today, an extensive park system covers nearly a quarter of the borough's surface, but by the twentieth century large sections of the Bronx had become home to legions of apartment dwellers. Since then, parts have become seriously blighted. The Bronx Green-up Program aims at reversing that trend through ongoing gardening projects. While the effort has had nowhere near the success, and nowhere near the support either, of Singapore's Green City movement, it has an inventory of 325 community greening projects as well as composting programs. Despite the community enthusiasm and widespread support, in 1999 it appeared that 114 community gardens located on land belonging to the City of New York were headed for the auction block. They were saved through behind-the-scenes work by garden staff and board members, along with support from the Trust for Public Land and a $1.2 million gift from singer Bette Midler. Since then twelve more gardens have been transferred to the Park Departments for preservation.

Walk back from the Family Garden through the forest, take the tram back, or circle the long way round on Magnolia Way, which is particularly lovely in April when twenty-five different types of magnolia bloom.

Having done all this, you have by no means exhausted the Garden's possibilities. The Rock Garden and Native Plant Garden are definitely worth some time. From the main entrance, you can find them by proceeding straight ahead down Rock Garden Path.

Turn left at the gate (there is a small admission fee) for the Rock Garden. This was the baby of T.H. Everett, a Kew-trained horticulturist. He came to the Garden in 1932 as director of horticulture, on condition that he be

Building the beloved Rock Garden.
From the archives of The LuEsther T. Merz Library, NYBG.

allowed to replace the small rock garden which existed at the time with something more interesting. He chose a depression between two rock out-croppings, and brought in rocks, big and little, from elsewhere in the garden. Because the Bronx in the summer is so unlike most mountain habitats, Everett ingeniously set up concrete basins under a slope so that water could circulate in them and cool the roots of the alpine plants. The plants themselves were set in gravel, which is not unlike the glacial debris they might grow in naturally. Other plants from dry, less frigid mountain areas grow in scree, or in sandy soil, while still others are clustered around a waterfall and watercourse. The garden underwent some major repairs in 1988, but is slated for more work, says the Garden's current master plan. It is, the plan says, "one of the great jewels" of the Garden.

The Native Plant Garden is a one hectare (2.5 acre) site set aside in memory of Elizabeth Knight Britton. In addition to her interest in mosses, she later became one of the founding members of the Wildflower Preservation Society, which is why a garden named after her and devoted to the native plants of the American Northeast is particularly appropriate.

LOST PLANTS

This little garden offers varied conditions, so that plants which evolved in quite different habitats can be grown in the same relatively small space. Among the plants is one which had disappeared for a hundred years. *Shortia galicifolia* was first discovered in the North Carolina hills by André Michaux, the intrepid French botanist who spent twelve years in North America and sent thousands of specimens to the Jardin des Plantes in the late 1700s.

In 1839 Asa Gray found the dried specimen in the Jardin's herbarium when studying North American specimens for his work on the flora of the Northeast U.S. It was unnamed so, in fine Linnaean fashion, he gave it the genus name *Shortia* after the Kentucky botanist Dr. Charles Wilkin Short. When he returned home Gray organized two expeditions to look for it in the wild, in 1841 and 1843, but with no luck.

His quixotic quest became a bit of a botanical joke, since Gray was otherwise one of the preeminent botanists of his day. But in 1877 a seventeen-year-old North Carolinian named George McQ. Hyams turned up the plant. He showed it to family friends who were amateur botanists, and who recognized that it was something quite rare but which they could not identify. They forwarded it to Gray, who identified it as Michaux's lost plant. Two years later Gray mounted another trip to the cool mountains of North Carolina, where young Hyams led him to the wild stands of *Shortia*. Since then more sites have been found, and this glossy-leafed, evergreen plant, which blooms in late spring with white fringed blossoms, is now commonly called Oconee Bells. In part of its range it is considered an endangered species, but it is also grown as a garden plant elsewhere.

Shortia is just one of many delights in the Native Plant Garden. Another is the meadow, which is mowed once in the fall around the end of November when all the flowers have developed seeds. It also is mowed twice in late April or early May in order to cut plants back and encourage branching, so that the plants will not topple over after being pelted by heavy rain. A final mowing is done with a push mower to cut pathways through the plants. The result is a flowering spectacle from early spring through autumn.

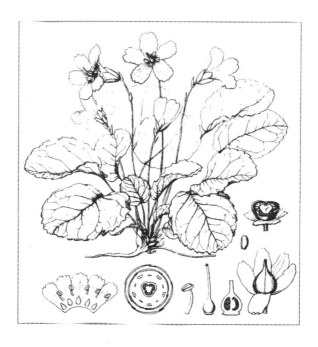

The rare *Shortia galicifolia*, or Oconee Bells, was first
discovered in the North Carolina hills by French botanist
André Michaux in the late 1700s.
Drawing by Charles E. Faxon, 1888.

The new master plan calls for giving this lovely garden its own entrance so that it will be less likely to be overlooked by visitors who may stop their exploration of this section once they have viewed the Rock Garden.

The Rock Garden and the Native Plant Garden are among the few which do not now bear the name of a benefactor. (In the Garden's older publications, the Rock Garden is called the T.H. Everett Rock Garden after its designer and founder but recently the name has been omitted.) One of the ways to raise funds for needed improvement is to name the project after one or more major donors.

FUNDING

Fund-raising from private sources has become increasingly important to the NYBG, particularly since severe cuts in government funding in the early 1990s brought on some hard times at the Garden. In 1987 government support provided slightly less than half of the budget or $7,195,000 while private support accounted to only 16 percent. By 1992, however, government support had dropped to less than a third of the garden's budget. To fill the gap industrious fundraising brought in $7,234,000, or 35 percent of the budget. By the end of the 1990s, government support had risen. It once again reached the $7.8 million mark in 2000, but instead of covering half the Garden's revenues it amounted to less than a quarter.

The moral, says the Garden's plan for 2001-2007, is that the Garden should not rely too much on any particular source of funding. Private donations are always harder to find in rough economic times, but they are indirectly subsidized in the United States (and Canada, but not the U.K., France, or Singapore) by governments since gifts to charitable foundations like the Garden receive tax credits. A change in this system to a "flat tax" on income, which is seriously advocated by some politicians, could wreak havoc by eliminating a major incentive for giving.

Relying on donations also presents the problem summed up in the proverb, he who pays the piper calls the tune. The New York Botanical Garden has been lucky from its beginnings not only to have friends with great fortunes, but also to have those fortunes derive from sources which are not in conflict with the evolving mission of a great botanical garden. As the Missouri Botanical Garden has discovered, accepting support from sources like Monsanto can call into question a botanical garden's independent status.

The difficulties the NYBG has met and overcome in recent years throw into deep relief the double conundrum that botanical gardens face. How is society to support the research necessary to safeguard our green world? And how can we fulfill our thirst for contact with that natural beauty?

The New York Botanical Garden provides corners
to contemplate nature.
Photo by Mary Soderstrom.

*Gardens of the
Twentieth Century*

In 1920 Brother Marie-Victorin became director of the department
of botany at the newly-formed Université de Montréal. As early
as 1925 he called for the creation of a botanical garden.
Courtesy of the Jardin Botanique de Montréal.

A Garden to Educate and Delight a Nation

THE STORY OF THE ORIGINS of the Jardin botanique de Montréal can be viewed as a lesson in how to turn bad times into good ones, and how people of vision can make a difference. The Jardin was built in the depths of the Great Depression of the 1930s as a make-work project. Its construction, however, would have been impossible if a Montreal cleric/botanist had not spent decades agitating for a botanical garden and if a forest specialist with the New York Botanical Garden had not already prepared detailed plans.

It is a good story, and one which may have implications for future of botanical gardens. To fully appreciate it though, you need to know a little about Montreal, Canada's second largest city and the *Métropole* of French Canada. It sits on an island in the middle of the St. Lawrence River, which drains perhaps twenty per cent of the North American continent including the entire Great Lakes basin. The springs are short, the summers are hot, the autumns are gorgeous, and the winters—well, the winters are what define the place.

In a good year Montreal receives about 200 centimeters, or more than eighty inches, of snow. Any time from the end of October until the middle of April the sky may fill with swirling flakes and white suddenly cover the landscape. For at least two months every winter, and often much longer, snow is what you see when you look outside, what you trudge through on the street, what you shovel when you want to drive your car.

The climate is much, much better than it was a few thousand years ago, however. The region was glaciated several times, so that the land was scoured down to bedrock in some places. Mount Royal, the large hill that gives the city its name, is a volcanic plug, remnant of an ancient seismic hotspot. If it ever were an active volcano, the evidence has long since been pushed south into New York State and Vermont by advancing glaciers.

Once the glaciers melted they left another legacy—huge inland seas and lakes whose traces can be seen in the flat land which forms the St. Lawrence Valley today. Successive shorelines left their mark—ancient waves cut beaches which form terraces today on the sides of Mount Royal. The Jardin botanique de Montréal sits just at the flat edge of one. From the southern edge of the Jardin on a clear day you can see the mighty river making its way northeast to the Atlantic as well as the city and suburbs, and beyond, three of the Monteregian Hills, which are more volcanic plugs streamlined by the flow of glaciers.

As the last Ice Age ended, and the climate moderated, the region's forests and rivers filled with fish and game. Native North Americans found excellent hunting and fishing, and by the time Europeans arrived they had established thriving communities at several places in the St. Lawrence Valley. In 1535 the French explorer Jacques Cartier made it this far up the river, nearly 500 kilometers (300 miles) from the Gulf of St. Lawrence. Samuel de Champlain returned several times in the early 1600s, and convinced King Louis XIII of France to sponsor a colony on the shores of the river in 1620.

OUTPOST OF THE FRENCH EMPIRE

Montreal itself, claims a birthdate of 1642. The location was a logical one since ships could go no further up the river due to of a series of treacherous rapids and ungovernable currents. Well into the nineteenth century fur traders set off in huge canoes from here for the Great Lakes and beyond. Canals and railroads (the first in a British colony) were built early on to transport goods to the outside world.

In 1763, what is now Canada, passed from French to English hands. Since then, the English and French have lived side by side in Montreal, sometimes as strangers, sometimes as friends. The city has also been the gateway to North America for hundreds of thousands of immigrants from around the world. Le Jardin botanique de Montréal profits from the cross-fertilizatin of ideas produced by the legacies of two grand European traditions, its rich immigrant traditions, as well as Montreal's proximity to the United States.

Today the seventy-two hectares (180 acres) of the Jardin botanique form a garden not as big as either the Royal Gardens at Kew or the New York Botanical Garden, but like both of them, it offers more than you can see in a day of exploring. One strategy in summer is to take the sightseeing tram which leaves near the Visitor Centre and stops at several places around the garden. Seeing the garden on foot, though, has its advantages. Not only are you close enough to the plants to smell them, but also to the explanatory material posted in each section.

Don't be afraid to visit during the snowy months. The contrast between the cold outside and the warmth of the greenhouses is a particular delight in winter, while walking or cross country skiing when the sun glints off the snow is an experience not encountered in many gardens elsewhere.

But suppose the visitor arrives anytime between spring and late fall. The main entrance to the Jardin (once you pass through the rather ugly turnstiles) is a grand, European-inspired vista leading toward the main administration building. Along the way, formal parterres are brilliant in late summer with annuals, while in spring they are filled with tulips and daffodils. To the right, beyond a screen of conifers, rises the tower of the Olympic Stadium, built for the 1976 Olympics. Called the Big O (or "Big Owe"), Montrealers are still paying for it twenty-five years later. The Olympic complex, with its huge cost overruns and facilities which prove unsuited for the community's needs, is a constant reminder of how public projects can go wrong.

MARIE-VICTORIN: VISIONARY

The statue which stands in front of the conifers is of Brother Marie-Victorin. This garden was his brainchild. Born Conrad Kirouac in 1885, Marie-Victorin was a member of the Christian Brothers teaching order and a devoted, committed naturalist. The Jardin was the logical extension of his belief in the importance of the natural sciences in educating both students and the general public, and in the necessity of having a beautiful and accessible place in which to study and enjoy nature.

Until the 1920s, the natural sciences had been neglected in French Canada. Education had long been "classical," aimed at preparing an elite group of men for careers as clerics, lawyers and physicians. While the curriculum contained enough science to prepare some men for medical studies, there was precious little emphasis on science for others. Marie-

Victorin deplored this. As early as 1925 he called for the creation of a botanical garden where science could develop concretely and where the general public could learn about and appreciate the plants of the region. He had already become a well-known educator with many published notes on the flora of the Laurentian mountains to his credit. Although he was self-taught as a botanist, he became the director of the botany department at the newly-formed Université de Montréal in 1920.

A First Attempt

The idea of establishing a botanical garden in Montreal was not new. In 1863, at a time when the botanical gardens in Singapore and St. Louis were brand new, and well before the first attempt to set up a modern garden in New York, Sir William Dawson of McGill College attempted to convince his board of governors to set up a garden, with help from Kew. Nothing came of that, but in the 1880s a botany club arranged for "the site where the earliest spring flowers bloom" on Mount Royal to be selected for a garden.

Frederick Law Olmsted, who designed Central Park with Calvert Vaux, had recently presented his plan for the development of Mount Royal as a public park. His proposal emphasized the rugged quality of the mountain's rocky outcrops. Shade trees would predominate at the lower elevations, but as a gently rising carriage road climbed to the top they would give place to coniferous trees. At the summit scrubby pines, firs, thorns, and other low vegetation would make the top even more "wild and forbidding," Olmsted said. He did not want what he called "floral embroidery" or flower beds because he believed they would would diminish the natural beauty of place. Flowering plants would grow, seemingly at random, in hundreds of small places, where "the original Gardener of Eden will delight your eyes with little pictures within greater pictures of indescribable loveliness." But due to the economic downturn following the Panic of 1873, Olmsted's plan was shelved although the carriage road was built.

Ten years later the botany club's garden seemed to get to a good start with a small appropriation from the city. Nearly 3,000 plants were collected, many of them gifts from other botanical gardens as far away as Coimbra in Portugal, Kew, and the Royal Botanic gardens in Saint Petersburg, Russia. Some of the plants were actually set out. But records show that two years later the land was being rented back to the city of Montreal. What caused

In 1932 Brother Marie-Victorin went to New York to offer Henry Teuscher
the position of head horticulturalist.
Courtesy of the Jardin Botanique de Montréal.

the abandonment of the project is not clear, but obviously the time was
not right.

Forty years passed before another serious attempt was made to
establish a botanical garden. By the 1930s, Brother Marie-Victorin, who
visited thirty-three botanical gardens following the 1929 International
Botanical Convention in Cape Town, South Africa, was assiduously lining
up support for the project and looking for someone to help him plan it. In
Henry Teuscher, a German landscape architect who had worked in several
botanical gardens and who was chief tree scientist at the New York Botanical
Garden, he found the ideal person.

HENRY TEUSCHER'S MISSION

In the spring of 1932 Brother Marie-Victorin went to New York to meet
Teuscher to ask if he would be interested in becoming head horticulturist
for a new garden. Teuscher immediately answered "Yes" enthusiastically,
but after some reflection he decided he had to refuse because the salary
offered for the fledgling project was too small. He wrote Marie-Victorin:

"I agreed (to work on the project)....because the vision which I had of your garden attracted me so immensely that I could hardly see anything else for the moment." Even though Teuscher could not accept, he kept thinking about the garden and offered to look over the first architects' plans. He immediately wrote back to Brother Marie-Victorin that they would not do. "Yours is the first botanical garden to be laid out after more than a generation. Yours is the chance to learn from all the mistakes of others," he wrote. "Please, do not repeat them, let me help you. I do not believe that I could bear it to see you miss the opportunity which you have got to lay out a botanical garden as perfect as it can be made with our present knowledge."

With devotion and enthusiasm, Teuscher continued to work on the design of the garden, corresponding frequently with Marie-Victorin and collaborating with the architects on the siting of buildings. It was another two years, however, before Teuscher actually visited Montreal. In the meantime he arranged for 10,000 trees and shrubs from the recently-dismantled Boyce Thompson Arboretum in New York to be given to Montreal's new garden and planted at a temporary location.

In 1935, with plans for the Jardin well advanced and academic accolades showering on him for *Flore laurentienne*, his definitive book about the flora of the Laurentian region, Marie-Victorin had another chance at getting the public money necessary to start construction on the Jardin in earnest. His old friend Camilien Houde was re-elected Mayor of Montreal, and preparations for the city's tricentennial celebrations were getting underway. On that happy occasion, "you will have to present a gift to the city, to your city," he wrote Houde. "But Montreal is ...a lady, and you can't offer her any old thing; a sewer system, a police station... So, for heaven's sake, pin flowers to her bosom, fill her arms with Roses and with all the Lilies of the Fields."

Convincing arguments, evidently. It helped also that both federal and provincial governments were setting up make-work programs to counter the massive unemployment of the Great Depression which was reaching its depths. Now there was money to hire Teuscher, and by the beginning of 1937, with the plans finally completed, more than half a million dollars had been promised by the governments, and 3,000 men were at work. "Since the plans were ready, we started work simultaneously on both ends as well as the in the middle," Teuscher wrote later.

Costs would rise to $11 million by 1940, an enormous sum for the

Construction of the main entrance, 1938.
Courtesy of the Jardin Botanique de Montréal.

Aerial view, 1948.
Courtesy of the Jardin Botanique de Montréal.

time. It was spent chiefly on the wages of the workers who, equipped with not much more than shovels, transformed what had been part of a rather pedestrian park into a garden designed to inspire everyone.

The formal entrance with its gorgeous display of flowers was part of Teuscher's original vision. Beauty, he believed, should be the bait which lures people to all botanical gardens. The administration building at the end of the vista also symbolized the new departures Teuscher planned. Designed in the Art Deco style that was introduced in France in the 1920s, it turned its back on the neo-gothic and Victorian gingerbread buildings which had become clichés of botanical garden construction.

Many of the administration building's details have been preserved during recent renovations, including the polychrome bas-reliefs of figures from the history of Montreal which run across the facade. Today, however, it is not a focal point of a visitor's experience in the garden. In good weather people want to see the more than thirty thematic gardens found throughout the Jardin's vast expanse, while in bad weather, the main attraction is the complex of greenhouses.

Tulip.
Emanuel Sweerts. *Florilegium,* 1612.

TULIPS

Suppose, though, that you're visiting on a warm May day when the tulips are in bloom. There is an abundance of them, fringed and plain, in splendid reds, yellows, oranges, and purples. Tulips became extravagantly popular in Europe, particularly in Holland, in the seventeenth century, but their origins lie in the highlands of Turkey. This Turkish connection is celebrated in one of the Jardin's newest features, the elegant mixture of artifact and flower of the Peace Garden courtyard just south of the restaurant. Its nine low walls and nine pillars are decorated with Iznik tiles in floral, particularly tulip, designs.

The tiles were produced in the Turkish city of Iznik, by a technique which dates back a thousand years. Lost from around 1750 until 1995, the process was redeveloped by the Iznik Foundation, which was established by Turkish archeologists and financial institutions in the early 1990s specifically to rediscover it. Now the foundation, the Jardin, and the Turkish community of Montreal have collaborated to produce this courtyard garden which invites the visitor to contemplate tulips on tiles even out of season.

On the other side of the restaurant begins the long series of exhibition gardens where bright colours vibrate against every conceivable shade of green during the summer and early fall. From the restaurant's terrace you will see the kind of vista European gardens are famous for: a sequence of gardens, arbors, fountains, and pergolas extending a quarter of a kilometer.

Exhibition Flower Beds

The sections devoted to annuals and perennials which thrive in the Montreal climate change each year as the Jardin experiments with new cultivars and new concepts in gardening. In the 1990s, for example, a wide range of ornamental grasses shared beds with yellow and orange rudbeckia and other late-season splendours. In the summer of 2000, eight new sorts of dahlias and three new impatiens in red, purple, and pink were on display, while nearby eight city gardens showed ways to solve the problems of limited space faced by every city gardener.

The exhibition beds are not all displays of flowers, though. An extensive section is devoted to economic plants, everything from tobacco through the many members of the *brassica* family (cabbage, cauliflower, broccoli, and many others) to different varieties of corn. The explanatory material is well-presented. The surprised look on children's faces when they realize that popcorn comes from a plant and not from a microwaveable container can alone be worth a visit to the Jardin.

The exhibition beds were among the first developed when the garden opened with aim of both delighting and educating. Teuscher believed strongly that the "ideal modern botanical garden" must include education. Indeed it was this broad public education aspect that he, like Marie-Victorin, considered the major difference between older botanical gardens and what

161

Rudbeckia laciniata.
Drawing by Nicolas Robert.

he wanted to create. "Modern man, living in the artificial desert of stone we call a city, has come more and more frequently to consider the plants, tree, bushes, and flowers which he sees in the public parks and along the avenues as pure ornaments," he wrote in the 1930s. The goal of the botanical garden should be to attract not only people who are interested in plants, but those who are actually indifferent to them. The garden should demonstrate why the natural world should be appreciated.

In many respects Marie-Victorin and Teuscher succeeded. From the time the first section of the Jardin was opened to the public in 1937, some Sundays saw as many as 15,000 visitors. Today more 20,000 visit on the May weekend designated "Le rendezvous horticole" when they can talk to experts from the Jardin and the region's horticultural companies. During an average year about a million visitors enjoy the Jardin.

ALPINE GARDEN

Across the road from the exhibition beds is the Alpine Garden, which sits on the flanks of the highest point in the Jardin. Since the parklands from which the garden was formed were originally quite flat, all the hills and dales, as well as the ponds, are man-made. Montreal lies only a few hundred feet above sea level, so you might expect the Alpine Garden's to look unconvincing. However, skillful design has created a credible mountainous setting. A stream cascades down the side of the hill, and the rocky, southward-facing slope is dotted with a wide variety of plants from the mountain regions of the world. The Alpine garden was one of the features which Teuscher insisted on, but which did not come into its own until after Expo 67, the International Exposition marking Canada's centenary in 1967. Alpine plants featured in the Canadian Pavilion were moved to the Jardin when Expo ended.

Just to the east of the Alpine Garden is a service complex consisting of greenhouses and beds used for research and for propagation and storage of plants. (The Jardin is also home to nearly a hectare [2.5 acres] of greenhouses used by the City of Montreal to grow plants for Montreal's public places. Located at the extreme north part of the Jardin, these green houses produce a million flowering plants of 230 varieties each year.)

South of this service complex is the series of ten exhibition greenhouses. Teuscher had planned to place exhibition greenhouses in this part of the Jardin, and shortly after the work on the Jardin got underway, a budget of

$100,000 was allocated for a heating plant and a greenhouse to display plants that cannot grow in Montreal's climate. Construction began, but the project fell victim to bad timing and bad luck. Canada entered World War II in September 1939, as did the rest of the British Empire. Around the same time there was a change in the provincial government which brought to power some ferocious enemies of the Jardin. Teuscher, despite the fact that he'd spent most of his adult life in North America and was an American citizen, became a convenient target, and was accused of being a German spy. He was eventually cleared and he continued to work toward completion of the Jardin's master plan, but he kept a much lower profile thereafter.

The new government attacked the Jardin as a waste of money, going so far as to seize the half-completed greenhouse and demolish it. During this period the federal government seriously considered requisitioning the garden for use by the Royal Canadian Air Force. It took all Marie-Victorin's persuasive arguments and diplomatic skills to see that the Jardin survived intact. Besides finding more friends in high places, he also opened the Jardin to hundreds of Victory Gardens plots where citizens grew vegetables for their own use and to relieve wartime food shortages; it was a project quite in keeping with his philosophy of involving people in the world of nature.

Then, suddenly, he was no longer there to pilot the Jardin through this tough period. In July 1944 he was killed in an automobile accident returning from a field trip in rural Quebec. His death was a shock to those around him, and a near tragedy for the Jardin. The botanists who were next in line to succeed him had clashing personalities and strongly differing ideas of where the Jardin should go. The Jardin suffered from lack of strong leadership for several years.

It was not until the 1950s that the Jardin could think of building exhibition greenhouses again. By then Teuscher was thoroughly behind the scenes (he continued to work for the botanical garden until he was in his seventies.) Three long-awaited central exhibition greenhouses were finally opened in 1956, and the rest were constructed over the next few years. They are home to a stunning collection of plants from different climates as well as exhibits on themes that often attract large crowds.

NOAH'S ARK AND OLIVES

"Noah's Ark" has been featured in several recent exhibits in the main greenhouse, comparing the pressing need to safeguard our planet's bio-

The Marsh and Bog Garden is considered one of
Henry Teuscher's most original ideas.
Photo by Mary Soderstrom.

diversity with the way Noah saved two of everything during the biblical
flood. During the summer of 2001, some of the plants which have helped
humankind over the ages were highlighted, among them papyrus, grains,
the cancer-curing Madagascar periwinkle, and the tree whose branch Noah's
dove brought back when the floodwaters were receding, the olive. Olives, a
staple food all around the Mediterranean, were also to be featured in
activities as the Jardin explored the mythology, history, archeology, and
cuisine of the Mediterranean region.

Each year the Jardin's greenhouses also welcome thousands of children
during the Great Pumpkin Ball. Kids get a chance to carve their own jack o'
lanterns and have them displayed in the main greenhouse and the visitors'
centre. Also on display are enormous squashes, pumpkins, and gourds,
grown in the garden and demonstrating the great variety found in this
plant family.

East of the greenhouses is the Rosearie, a sumptuous collection of
10,000 roses which bloom from June through mid-October. This garden
devoted to the queen of flowers alone would be enough to attract the visitor
to this part of the Jardin, but the Jardin's eastern section also contains some
of its most unusual features. One of them is the Bog and Marsh garden

right next to the Rosearie. The garden is composed of 110 concrete basins in which grow water lilies, rushes and other water plants rarely so attractively displayed. Nearby benches invite the visitor to sit down and listen to the many fountains or watch the dragon flies zip over the surface of the ponds. This garden is considered to be one of Teuscher's most original designs, and has been maintained more or less as he conceived it.

Indeed it is a tribute to the completeness and originality of Teuscher's master plan for the Jardin that no major deviations from what he laid out were undertaken until well into the 1970s. Then in the northern part of the Jardin, an old quarry which he had foreseen as a combination hanging garden and geological exhibit, was filled in. Since the grand formal collection of trees Teuscher had planned as an arboretum had never been completed, the arboretum was expanded to include the quarry site. It now covers forty hectares (ninety-eight acres), or more than half the Jardin, and contains some 7,000 trees and shrubs. Nearly every variety that grows in Montreal's climate is present, grouped according to species.

While the woods are marvelous to walk through, and great for bird watching, this section of the Jardin was somewhat under-visited until the Tree House was added in 1996. This interpretation centre features permanent and temporary exhibits with wood and the woods as a theme. "Musical Wood: From Trees to Instruments" was the title of one show that included displays of wooden musical instruments like recorders, harpsichords, hurdy-gurdies, guitars, and the entire violin family, as well as demonstrations of how to construct and play them. The olive tree was to be featured in 2001-2 with an exhibit detailing its cultural and culinary importance.

In early spring every year, the Tree House also throws a huge Quebec-style sugaring-off party, with traditional music, boiling maple sap, and *tire d'érable* or hot maple syrup that becomes candy when poured on clean, packed snow.

Two other spectacular and recent additions to the Jardin, the Insectarium and the Butterfly House, sit in the eastern section of the Jardin.

INSECTS

The connection of insects to plants is obvious; many plants rely on insects to pollinate them. Yet the inclusion of a museum, the Insectarium, devoted to insects in a botanical garden has raised more than a few eyebrows. Pierre

Bourque, director of the Jardin from 1980 until 1994 when he was elected mayor of Montreal, was responsible for initiating this project. He had met Georges Brossard, a serious amateur insect collector who was trying to find a way to make his enormous collection of insects from all around the world accessible to the public. Together they found sponsors and other collectors looking for a place to display their collections. The result is an exuberant educational program, sometimes even offering edible cooked insects as delicacies. The Insectarium, housed in a building with a swooping roof that opened in 1990, attracts about 400,000 visitors a year. Next to the Insectarium a net-enclosed flyway is home to butterflies from June to September. In the summer of 1999 it received 75,000 visitors.

Bourque's vision, energy, and devotion to the Jardin resembles that of Marie-Victorin and Teuscher. Even those who criticize his record as mayor of Montreal recognize the quality of the work he did at the Jardin. A horticulturist by training, he went to work for the City of Montreal, fresh from his studies, during Expo 67. He came to the Jardin shortly before the 1976 Olympics opened, and was responsible for the planning of Floralies 1980, a sort of horticultural Olympics with floral exhibits prepared by countries around the world which was held on an island in the St. Lawrence.

JAPANESE AND CHINESE GARDENS

Contacts made during that international floral exposition led Bourque to Japan and China and to plans, sponsored by private individuals as well as governments, for Japanese and Chinese gardens. The former was opened in 1988, and combines stone and plants from Quebec with Japanese philosophy to create a garden which is both uniquely adapted to Montreal's climate and also true to the meditative traditions of a culture half-way around the world. A stream and pond with slow-moving, multi-coloured carp, or *Koi*, lies at the heart of the garden, which also contains cascades and springs symbolizing life and renewal. A collection of thirty Japanese minia-ture trees, or *bonsai*, some more than 300 years old, are displayed in the Japanese garden's cultural pavilion.

The Chinese garden, opened in 1991, also features miniature trees, called *penying*. But unlike the Japanese garden, much of this garden was actually built abroad. Its pavilions, bridges, and other architectural features were created in Shanghai, broken down into thousands of pieces, and then shipped to Montreal in 120 containers. It took fifty Chinese artisans nearly

The Jardin's Japanese Garden uses materials from Quebec
to express Japanese garden philosophy.
Photo by Mary Soderstrom.

a year to reassemble the elements.

Inspired by private gardens created in southern China during the Ming dynasty (1368-1644), the Chinese garden has become home to one of the Jardin's most popular activities, the annual Chinese lantern festival. During the early evenings of autumn, the Jardin stays open so visitors can see the magic of hundreds of shining lanterns. These vary from modest ones made from bamboo and paper to a two-meter long (7 foot) ceramic dragon which seems to float in the center of Dream Lake.

The Jardin also is home to noble examples of gardens in the great English tradition. To the north of the Japanese garden lie two ponds which were excavated in the original plan for the garden, where waterfowl make their homes today. The Flowery Brook sector presents a constantly changing display of flowers from early spring until fall. The heady smell of the large collection of lilacs fills the air in late spring. In the winter, cross-country ski trails invite Montrealers to enjoy the pleasures of a snowy country.

FIRST NATIONS GARDEN

Nearby is the Maple Grove and Spruce stand, which present five groups of trees typical of Quebec: hickory and sugar maple found around Montreal;

sugar maples, beeches, and American lindens from the Beauce and Québec City regions; yellow birch and maple from the Eastern Townships and the Laurentian Mountains; and conifers, represented by a white spruce grove and a pine grove of red, white, and jack pines. This section of the Jardin is being developed as the Garden of the First Nations, a tribute to the people who lived in Quebec before Europeans arrived, the Abenakis, Algonquins, Attikameks, Crees, Hurons-Wendats, Maliceets, Micmacs, Mohawks, Innu, Naskapis, and Inuit. It is scheduled to open in August 2001, as part of the celebrations of the 300th anniversary of the Peace of Montreal when the French settlers met with delegations of Native Canadians to sign a peace treaty. Montreal, called Ville Marie then, only had about 1500 inhabitants, while the First Nation delegations numbered about 1200 and came in 200 canoes.

Jacques Lincourt, the Jardin's current director, speaks enthusiastically about this project which is similar to one outlined in Teuscher's plans many years ago. Jacques Rousseau, one of the directors who succeeded Marie-Victorin, was also very interested in ethnobotany and did research in the homeland of the Naskapi First Nation in northeastern Quebec.

Lincourt began his horticultural career working with Pierre Bourque on Floralies 80. Since then Lincourt has not strayed far from the Jardin and seems to have Mayor Bourque's ear. Not such a bad thing, perhaps, when it comes ensuring that horticultural matters have a prominent place on the city's agenda. The Bourque administration has experienced some rough times—economic stagnation and conflicts with city workers, to name only two—but the city has continued to present a flower-bedecked face to the world through street plantings and displays of annual flowers throughout its public spaces. It is not as green as Singapore by a long shot, but neither is it the gray northern city it might easily become given the short growing season.

The Jardin has not been immune to budget cuts. Lincourt says that municipal financing remained steady until the 1980s, when $2.3 million was cut from the Jardin's $16 million budget. That was just at the moment when Bourque was steering the Jardin toward ambitious new projects like the Japanese and Chinese gardens. In order to make up the shortfall, the garden was forced to commercialize somewhat. An entrance fee for the greenhouses was first charged in 1985. Then in 1991, after the opening of the Chinese Garden, the charge was extended to anyone entering the

grounds during the high season. (Those who want to consult the horticultural service or do research in the library have the fee refunded.)

The Jardin also now rents out its facilities. For $100 and the cost of
entrance fees for all members of the wedding party, you can have your
wedding pictures taken in the greenhouses. Or you can rent a greenhouse
or reception room for a party or meeting. In 2001 use of all ten greenhouses
plus the reception center for an evening costs $5,500.

"We have not become Disney World," asserts Lincourt, "but we have
tried to make the garden a popular place. And in order to attract people
you must give them ambiance; you have to make the exhibits dynamic."
Take the exhibit on olives and Mediterranean vegetation, as an example. It
is to feature food tasting—olives, to be sure, but also samples of other
plants from the region including grapes, rosemary, and oregano. Associations of people whose roots are in the Mediterranean region were to be
involved too, just as Chinese and Japanese Quebecers have become sponsors
and planners of activities in their respective gardens.

The effort has paid off. Attendance figures have kept up despite the
entrance fee and increasing competition for the recreation-tourist dollar
from other attractions like the new science facility at Montreal's Old Port.
This is extremely important. The Berlin Botanical Garden, whose plant
collection is about the same size as the Jardin's, has seen attendance drop
to about 300,000 a year. Not only has this meant declining revenues, it also
means that the Berlin Botanical Garden is perceived as less important and
so less worthy of support from other sources.

At the turn of the twenty-first century, the Jardin was receiving about thirty
percent of its budget from non-governmental sources like entrance fees.
However, it was apparent that not much of this came from private
donations. Unlike the gardens in St. Louis or New York, few of the Jardin's
special features bear the names of individual or corporate *mécènes*, or
philanthropists.

Lincourt explains: "We don't have the philanthropic tradition that other
places have, and so we're going to have to work at that." The Fondation
Marie-Victorin was set up in 1993 to benefit the botanical garden and
Insectarium, as well as two other popular scientific centers in Montreal,
the Planetarium and Biodôme. (The latter, an enclosed habitat featuring
the plants and animals of four different ecosystems, is found not far from

Brother Marie-Victorin at the Jardin. Public education and the involvement of children was a priority from the garden's early days.
Service des archives, Université de Montréal, Fonds Jules Brunel.

the Jardin in the former Olympic grounds. Pierre Bourque says he always considers the Biodôme as an extension of the Jardin since it is concerned with the same things.) The foundation is actively seeking corporate financing, but sponsorships are being carefully considered before being accepted. Lincourt says that while there is no problem with having a certain kind of milk featured in the restaurant, for example, the garden turned down the offer of a supermarket chain to support one project because the company did not have a policy of buying local produce. Encouraging local agriculture is part of the garden's overall commitment to a green world.

Conservation, along with education and research, is one of the Jardin's primary roles. Information about endangered species is included in many displays and handouts. The Jardin conducts workshops about Quebec's endangered indigenous plants with scientists, botanists, landscape architects, and producers of food and ornamental plants.

As for research, at the beginning of the new century the Jardin and its university partners were in the process of rethinking their priorities and protocols. After Marie-Victorin's death, the garden's scientific mission had more than its share of ups and downs. Strong personality conflicts as well as unclear relationships with universities led to many changes over the years, and to a few dramatic resignations. Since 1990, the *Institut de recherche en biologie végétale* has provided the structure for cooperative work by biologists, using the Jardin's facilities and drawing on the resources found in the region's universities.

Many of the current research projects are based firmly in a desire to manage the world in a more ecologically sound manner. In one of them a small ecosystem of marsh and other plants treats the waste water from the nearby Biodôme.

Another project is attempting to propagate temperate zone orchids from seed. Unlike the tropical orchids, with which Singapore has had such excellent results, orchids from the forests of the temperate zones have resisted propagation by nurseries or botanical gardens. They are lovely plants which many people want to grow. The result has been enormous pressure on them in their natural setting, to the point of endangering many species. Montreal scientists are using the pink lady's slipper (*Cypripedium acaule*) to study what chemical or physical conditions affect germination rates of the orchid seeds.

But it is the Jardin and its plants which matters in the eyes of most of the people who use it. More than half of the visitors come from the Montreal area, while ten percent are from the rest of Quebec. That means that only slightly more than a third of all visitors are from elsewhere in Canada or other countries. It also means that Marie-Victorin's aim of providing a beautiful place which would educate and inspire his fellow citizens has been in large measure achieved.

The Jardin botanique de Montréal belongs to the wider world. In size, quality of collection, and beauty, it is one of the best—and a great example of how individual commitment to an ideal can benefit the world.

Plants from Mediterranean climates grow outside in the
Strybing Arboretum and Botanical Garden.
Photo by Mary Soderstrom.

The Flowers of San Francisco

SPRING ARRIVES in late February or early March in San Francisco. Fly into the Bay Area from the still-wintry East, and from the Sierra Nevada westward the hills are covered with what looks like green velvet. The grass is already green in San Francisco. The deciduous trees will be leafing out, and the magnolias and camelias will be in bloom. There is a good chance the days will be warm and clear so that the Berkeley and Oakland hills across the Bay will glisten in the sunlight, every detail fresh as a smogless morning. It is, some would say, the weather of paradise—not too hot, not too cold, and fragrant with flowers.

The Bay itself is formed where the combined flow of the Sacramento and San Joaquin Rivers have cut through twin ramparts of Coastal Range hills. On the east side of the bay the hills rise as high as 1173 meters (3849 feet) at Mt. Diablo, while on the west side Mt. Tamalpais stands 784 meters (2571 feet.) In between a mix of sea water and fresh fill a submerged valley that is 125 km (75 miles) long.

The face which the California coast presents to the Pacific Ocean is a bulwark not broken in many places. Unlike the flat lands bordering the Atlantic and the Gulf of Mexico where barrier islands and river mouths form frequent safe moorings, good ports are few and far between, and San Francisco is the very best of them. The city is built at the extreme end of the row of hills which form the southern side of the Golden Gate. Wind-swept, hilly, and suffused with constantly changing light, this is one of America's most beautiful cities.

By standards of western North America, it is also old. At the time when Montreal was beginning to grow accustomed to being governed from

England and not France, when the British Royals were beautifying Kew gardens, and when Leiden's gingko was just a sapling, California was being colonized by the Spanish. Franciscan fathers, under Juan Junipero Serra, established a series of twenty-one missions in California beginning in the 1770s. The first mass was celebrated at Mision de San Francisco de Asis just five days before the American Declaration of Independence was signed in July 1776.

Over the next seventy years, the European population grew slowly. Mexico wrested its independence from Spain in 1820, and following the Mexican-American War which ended in 1848, California became an American territory. But it was not until gold was discovered that year that migration to California began in earnest. Between 1848 and 1860 the European and American population catapulted from 15,000 to 380,000.

San Francisco was the gateway. From the beginning it was a city filled with high spirits and optimism. By 1870 it was the tenth largest city in the United States, and the city fathers were eager to make it a first-class place.

This included setting up parks. Kew was blooming under the guidance of Sir Joseph Hooker just then, and Central Park was the pride of New York City. (By 1865 the big park on Manhattan island was welcoming six million visitors a year.) Public parks, providing green refreshment for the bodies and souls of city-dwellers, were becoming a necessity for every well-run city.

Olmsted Thought it was Impossible

Frederick Law Olmsted, who designed Central Park with Calvert Vaux and who planned Mount Royal Park in Montreal, had spent part of the 1860s in California. His time at Yosemite in the Sierra Nevada mountains led him to become one of its champions and also a leader in the movement to establish national parks. He had also drawn plans (now lost) for the town of Berkeley across San Francisco Bay, and had designed a cemetery in the Oakland hills which familiarized him with what grows well in the dry summer and mild winters of the Bay area. He was the logical person to ask for advice in planning the new San Francisco park.

Olmsted was one of the most eloquent advocates for giving city-dwellers access to the natural world. A beautiful landscape, he wrote early in his career, "consists of combinations of trees, standing singly or in groups, and casting their shadows over broad stretches of turf, or repeating their beauty by reflection upon the calm surface of pools, and the predominant associations are in the highest degree tranquilizing and grateful." But Olmsted said frankly that he thought it would be impossible to create such a landscape on the land which had been earmarked for a park in San Francisco. Nearly three-quarters of the site was sand dunes and Olmsted advised starting over at a better location.

"There is not a full grown tree of beautiful proportions near San Francisco," he wrote, "nor have I seen any young trees that promised fairly, except, perhaps of certain compact clumpforms of evergreens, wholly wanting in grace and cheerfulness. It would not be wise nor safe to undertake to form a park upon any plan which assumed as a certainty that trees which would delight can be made to grow near San Francisco."

Reclaiming the Sand Dunes

But the city's young civil engineer William Hammond Hall was not so pessimistic. The 400 hectares (1000 acres) earmarked for the park contained 108 hectares (270 acres) that "may at once be converted into an attractive resort," he wrote in a report to the Park Commission in 1871. The rest—he agreed with Olmsted that it was "a waste of drifting sand"—nevertheless could be reclaimed in a few years' time "until the barren sand hills are converted into verdant fields."

Four months after starting work, he had 3000 trees ready to plant in the portions suitable for immediate planting, with plans to set out another

Plowing the sand dunes, 1871.
Courtesy of Strybing Arboretum and Botanical Garden.

17,000 in 1872. Three years later, blue gums (eucalyptus) were nearly six meters (about twenty feet) high and Monterey pines and Monterey cypress were more than four meters (about thirteen feet) high with a spread of three to four meters (about ten to twelve feet). Roads had been graded and glades created. But what was really astonishing was the way the waves of sand had been stopped from rolling eastward on the prevailing winds.

To do this, Hall began by creating a huge artificial dune of brush and walls along the Great Highway which formed the western boundary of the park and ran along the beach. The surfaces were planted with mat-forming grasses, including a sand grass (*Ammophila arenaria*) imported from France, and which were interplanted with barley. The seeds germinated within five days, and effectively checked sand drift in twelve days. Then the newly-stabilized dunes were planted with lupine and other plants, some of them imported, to create heaths. Massive windbreaks of pine, cypress, and eucalyptus were planted too, so that within six years young evergreens were established. By the time Hall stepped aside in 1887, the entire reserve had truly become a park.

But it was only a park, with neither an arboretum nor a botanical garden, although the eccentric millionaire James Lick had given it a conservatory in the 1870s. He had been much impressed by the Palm House at Kew, and had the Lord and Burnham Company of New York (which would later build the splendid conservatory at the New York Botanical Garden), construct one from redwood with a boiler which was shipped on a clipper ship around the tip of South America. (The glass house has been closed since 1995, undergoing a $20 million restoration.)

Development of a real botanical garden was still far in the future. John McLaren, the second Superintendent of Parks, noticed that an area in Golden Gate Park was designated as a future arboretum and as early as the 1890s began planting conifers there. His plan was based on that of the Arnold Arboretum at Harvard University, where plantings are grouped along taxonomic lines. This approach underlies parts of the Garden today since trees planted then still exist. But thirty years later the way opened toward the development of a full-fledged arboretum and botanical garden.

Helene Strybing, a wealthy widow, was the fairy godmother who made the current garden possible. When she died in 1926, she left her estate to the City of San Francisco, with an initial immediate bequest and the rest to come after the last of her siblings in Germany had died. Thus it was not until 1939 that complete sum of $200,000 came to the city. Well before then, however, park officials had begun planning.

Mrs. Strybing had very definite ideas of what sort of garden she wanted her money to buy, even though the botanical garden's official publications say that not much is known about why she set up her bequest the way she did or who counseled her. The garden, her will said, was "to contain especially a collection of trees, shrubs and plants indigenous to, or characteristic, of California. It is my wish that plants of California and also plants used for medical purposes, whether native of California or not, shall be given special consideration in this collection." She also specified that "all trees, shrubs and plants are to be properly labeled for purposes of information and instruction."

WPA HELPS BUILD NEW ARBORETUM AND GARDEN
In 1937 Eric Walther was appointed supervisor of the arboretum and plans were drawn up by him and Park Superintendent John McLaren after visits to a

Helene Strybing
Courtesy of Strybing Arboretum and Botanical Garden.

number of botanical gardens and arboreta around the United States. As in Montreal, city officials were able to turn bad times to some good end. The Works Progress Administration (WPA), that New Deal program which left a legacy of park and public-space construction all over the United States, was enlisted to build the garden. Work began in the fall of 1937 on a section of not quite a hectare (4.5 acres) that was formally opened in 1940. WPA-made maps still exist of the garden, drawn to two-foot scale, and showing a Garden of California and a medicinal garden that recall the original prototypes of botanical gardens from the sixteenth century.

The Strybing Arboretum and Botanical Garden today covers twenty-two hectares (fifty-five acres) on the western end of Golden Gate Park. Like the Jardin des Plantes in Paris, Strybing charges no admission and so it is impossible to say how many people visit in a year. But, says director Scot Medbury, surveys show that about 15 million visit Golden Gate Park in a year and it is safe to assume that a significant proportion visit Strybing.

The main entrance to the Garden is off one of Golden Gate Park's curving roads, Martin Luther King Drive, near the corner of Lincoln Way, the park's southern boundary. To the south San Francisco's signature attached houses, set out on a grid of streets which laugh at the city's topography, march up a hill. The University of California at San Francisco sits near the top. Its 42.8 hectare (107 acre) campus on Parnassus Heights is one of the world's best health training centers, and has been part of the university since the days Golden Gate Park was begun. The neighbourhood grew up between the great San Francisco earthquake in 1906 and the Second World War. It is residential, but it has a buzz about it that is peculiarly San Francisco.

The San Francisco County Fair Building sits on the corner. Opened in 1960 as the Hall of Flowers, it represents one of those clever little arrangements through which San Francisco sets itself apart. Agriculture has always been big business in California, and in the 1950s the State set up a fund to finance new county fair buildings. But there is practically no agriculture in San Francisco. To qualify for the funds, the large flower show held every August was declared a county fair, and the gallery, auditorium, and offices built to house it became fair buildings. The timing was ironically appropriate: in the following decade San Francisco and Golden Gate Park were to become the center for 1960s counter-culture and the home of thousands of Flower Children.

Today Strybing is part of the San Francisco Recreation and Park Department, but only about half the Garden's expenses are met by municipal grants. The rest comes from the Strybing Arboretum Society, an organization created in 1955 to conduct educational programs and to provide additional funding which would not fluctuate with the city's finances. The relationship between the society and the local government is very close. The County Fair Building houses the society's offices and educational pro-grams.

To enter the Garden, the visitor walks through wide, open gates and down a promenade between the Fair buildings and the Helen Russell Crocker Library to the left, and a fence which shelters a series of demonstration gardens to the right. At the end of the buildings lies the garden's main lawn with an enormous Monterey cypress guarding the vista. From the lawn you look toward fountains and across to the Zellerbach perennial garden with its gazebo on the other side of the swale.

Sometime in the not too distant future that vista and the garden entry's focus are going to change because the magnificent cypress is reaching the end of its natural life. Planted in 1872, it is already older than the 125 years a tree of the species usually lives, and in recent years it has lost several large limbs. But a garden is always a work in progress, says Director Scott Medbury, and as the century turned Strybing was in the process of a major reflection on its future, including a re-thinking of its master plan and the way it fits into Golden Gate Park as a whole. It was, Medbury says, the time to decide what stories the garden should tell in the future. To do so the garden was about to undertake a fundraising drive to prepare the way for the changes which will cost in the neighborhood of $40 million.

Not brought into question was the idea of capitalizing on San Francisco's mild Mediterranean climate with its winter rains and summer droughts. It is a climate where plants from all over the world can grow without protection; there are no exhibition glass houses at Strybing. Plants from the five regions called Mediterranean—California, the lands surrounding the Mediterranean Sea, the Western Cape of South Africa, central-coastal Chile, and Southern and Southwestern Australia—thrive here naturally. But also, given variations in micro-climate and with some irrigation, plants from mountainous parts of tropical America and Asia, as well as plants from temperate regions of Asia, Europe, New Zealand, and the Americas, do very well.

Right now, the experience you have in the Garden depends on whether you turn right or left as you enter. To the right, with an entrance almost hidden behind the bookstore and garden shop, are the demonstration gardens. There are several small distinct gardens, designed to show what can be done in a garden in the California climate. Opened officially in 1966, most of them were designed at least twenty years ago, and frequently the building materials and garden furniture featured are no longer readily available. Revitalization of these gardens is on the to-do list for the new Garden plan because encouraging the use of plants adapted to the local conditions is one of the Strybing garden's priorities. As Medbury says: "In much of California you can grow anything if you water it enough. You can have England even, but doing that is pretty irresponsible." In the meantime, the entrance to the demonstration gardens may be shifted forward to be nearer the Main Lawn, and thus easier to find.

AN AMBIANCE OF TREES

At the edge of the Main Lawn you can see the skyline of trees McLaren planted as windbreaks and shelter belts. Like the Lawn's cypress, many of them are reaching the end of their lives. As these big trees blow down or are removed, the plants growing under them will receive much more light, which will require adjustments. Planting new trees will also have short-term effects, because many of the trees which develop into giants with spreading canopies start out as squat conical shapes taking up much more ground space than do the mature trees. Fifty years from now the entire ambiance of the garden will be determined by the decisions made now about what sort of trees to plant.

An example of just what that means can be seen at the far end of the lawn on either side of the fountain. More than one hundred crabapples of twenty different varieties were planted there in 1964. By now they should provide clouds of pastel blossoms in the spring, billows of foliage in summer, and thousands of tiny red and orange fruits in the fall. But crabapples do not do as well in mild climates as they do in more severe ones, so the colour palette which had been planned did not materialize. A way to produce a similar effect would be to plant trees with silvery foliage— olives from the Mediterranean on the right, and *leucodendrons* from South Africa on the left, perhaps. The trees would also make a link between the Main Lawn and the geographic regions featured just beyond on either side.

The edge of the lawn is home, however, to a collection of flowering trees which are breathtaking in spring. Strybing's magnolia collection is one of the finest in the world, while its azaleas and rhododendrons provide clouds of colour when they bloom.

Rhododendron.
J. Foord. *Decorative Plant and Flower Studies*, 1906.

Just in front of the Library to the left of the entrance is the Asian Discovery Garden. It was dedicated in a ceremony with traditional Lion Dancers in the spring of 2000. From a small knoll you can look down on a collection of plants which provide a preview of the garden's larger Asian areas. Next to it is the Library Terrace Garden, which includes an outdoor garden room for the Helen Crocker Russell Library. The intimate space is arranged in an excavated hollow, the earth from which was used to build the knoll. A wall made from limestone blocks, remnants of a twelfth century Spanish monastery brought to the U.S. by William Randolph Hearst in the 1930s, encloses the garden.

There are many more of these blocks. Hearst had the monastery dismantled and the stones boxed, marked and shipped to California. He had intended to re-erect the structure on one of his estates, but offered it to the City of San Francisco after he ran into some business reverses. The City agreed, intending to rebuild it in Golden Gate Park. A fire destroyed the crating and the re-assembly instructions, and ever since the blocks sit in the park waiting to be put to some new use.

Some of the blocks were used to build the raised beds in the Garden of

Eric Walther, first director of the Strybing with
magnolia campbellii.

Fragrance, one of several small gardens within Strybing which are dedicated
to particular themes. Filled with aromatic plants like rosemary, lemon,
vebena, and lavender and labeled in Braille, the Garden of Fragrance lies
just off the path which goes around the right side of the Main Lawn. Nearby
is the Biblical Garden which features plants mentioned in the Bible or which
grew in the eastern Mediterranean during biblical times.

Continue to the right and you'll pass the path which leads to the top of
Heidelberg Hill. (The name is another leftover from Golden Gate Park's
past: the knoll was the site of the beer garden for a mid-winter fair in the
1890s.) From here you can get a grand view of more magnolias and some
of the 900 different varieties of rhododendrons grown at Strybing.

At the bottom of the hill lies the waterfowl pond, a favorite stop for
passing birds and bird lovers. At the pond's upper end lie the swampy walk-
ways of the Primitive Plant Garden. This unusual display brings together
living relatives of plant groups which once dominated the earth and most
of whose members are now known only in fossils—club mosses, true
mosses, ferns, horsetails, cycads, ginkgos, conifers and early flowering plants.
The garden is in effect a showroom for evolutionary theory. The afternoon
sunlight through the banana palms is a luscious green.

A bit further on the visitor comes to the Friend Gate entrance, and another vista of grass and water, with Grandview Hill in the distance. Golden Gate Park as a whole was planned to present both enclosed and open spaces, and here is one of Strybing's most lovely examples. People feel at home here. It is a textbook case of evolutionary psychology's outline of what landscapes humans came to favour. It is also just what Frederick Law Olmsted prescribed: "trees, standing singly or in groups, and casting their shadows over broad stretches of turf, or repeating their beauty by reflection upon the calm surface of pools." He would be surprised and probably pleased to see that such a landscape was fashioned from the sand dunes.

Plants from Down Under

If you continue to walk along the path which runs around the perimeter of the Garden, you will soon find yourself surrounded by plants originating in Eastern Australia. Many of them like bottle brush and various eucalyptus are familiar to anyone who has spent much time in California, because they have become mainstays of Pacific Coast landscaping.

Plants from New Zealand also have a strong presence at Strybing. As early as 1859 plants and seeds from there were imported by San Francisco nurserymen, and many New Zealand natives, like the red-flowered New Zealand Christmas tree (*Metrosideros excelsus*), became popular street trees. But it was the 1915 Panama-Pacific International Exhibition which brought a large number plants from New Zealand to San Francisco. Twenty-one countries built pavilions at the exhibition, which was held to celebrate the opening of the Panama Canal and the recovery of San Francisco from the disastrous 1906 earthquake and fire. The New Zealand pavilion was one of the most popular, with its display of massed tree ferns and many other exotic plants. Records show that after the Exposition was over 150 plants were transferred from the New Zealand building to Golden Gate Park. Of these, a substantial number were planted out in the section which became Strybing. Among them are a pukatea tree, now twelve meters (about forty feet) high, and one of the largest outside New Zealand. The New Zealand collection has grown steadily. Eric Walther, the first Strybing director, planned a significant section devoted to plants from that country, so acquisitions continued throughout the twentieth century. The New Zealand sector now is three-fifths of a hectare (two acres) near the center of the garden, south of the waterfowl pond where a thicket of Nikau palms grows.

The New Zealand collection highlights the truism that a garden is always changing, as successive visions enhance the accomplishments of earlier plans. But nowhere is that easier to see at Strybing than in the collections of Asian plants.

Strybing is home to two Japanese-influenced gardens. The Takamine Garden with its azaleas and flowering cherries is located on the south side, in the area which is broadly categorized as the main Asian section and just a short stroll from the Asian Discovery Garden near the entrance. The Moon Viewing Garden Pavilion, on the other hand, is west of the Friend Gate. This Japanese stroll garden features a wooden deck built out over water from which reflections (including the moon when the time is right) can be contemplated. Nearby a waterfall, landscaped in Japanese style, provides the soothing sound of water. This garden can be seen as the transition to a second, large section of Asian plants, the Southeast Asian Cloud Forest, which is on the rise just to the west.

It is fitting that San Francisco would have excellent Asian collections. This is the city which has turned toward the Pacific from its beginning. Chinese immigrants helped build it and the railroads which linked it to the Eastern United States. While the early treatment of these workers (and those from Japan and elsewhere in Asia) is a sorry chapter in California's history as it was elsewhere in North America. The triumph of their children and grandchildren in many fields—academia, business, sport, music, the arts—enriches the country and the world.

It is also appropriate that Strybing develop an area devoted to cloud forest ecosystems. San Francisco is one of the few places in the world where temperature and humidity match that of the mountains of tropical regions, since the fogs of Golden Gate Park are a good substitute for the clouds of higher elevations. Strybing's two cloud forests—the second one has plants from the mountains of Central America, and Mexico's Chiapas State—are an important link in the chain that anchors the concept of biodiversity to the real world.

"Ideally," says Bian Tan, Strybing's collections manager who has made plant conservation trips to tropical mountains, "plants should be conserved where they grow, as should their habitats. But growing threatened plants in botanical gardens is better than letting them go extinct. And if the plants can be reintroduced to their natural habitat, once measures have been taken to protect it, so much the better."

SAVING PLANTS FROM EXTINCTION

Bian Tan recounts how one plant, *Deppea splendens*, which has two-inch orange flowers hanging in long clusters, was discovered by a botanist from the California Academy of Sciences (which cooperates closely with Strybing and whose herbarium is used frequently by Strybing staff) growing exclusively in one canyon in Chiapas, Mexico. He brought seeds back to Strybing, where they have done very well. Seedlings are often available to home gardeners through regular Strybing plant sales. But the rescue was just in time. Since then, the canyon has been cleared for cornfields, and the shrub is assumed to be extinct in the wild.

Tan spent August of 1999 collecting plants in the mountains of the Philippines and on the island of Flores, near Timor in East Indonesia. With collaborators from the National Museum of the Philippines and the Bali Botanic Gardens, he traveled wet and muddy mountain roads to areas where endangered plants grow. Some of the country they visited was supposed to be protected from development but was in fact being turned into potato and cabbage fields. Nevertheless about 200 species were collected, most of them as cuttings. While some of the cuttings have not survived, most, including six extremely rare rhododendrons, are doing fine, and should be ready to be set out in the cloud forest in about three years. Duplicate plants will be grown and propagated at other botanical gardens, such as the one at the University of California at Berkeley.

But Strybing is not only concerned with collectiing plants from far away places. The John Muir Nature Trail winds through the westernmost part of the Garden. Along it the visitor will find plants that are native to the San Francisco region, some of which were collected from the last remaining pockets of native vegetation. One of them, *Ribes divaricata*, is considered extinct in the wild, but has been reintroduced to the places along the nature trail where it formerly grew.

Conservation efforts along the trail benefit more than plants. California quail used to be abundant in the area, with coveys of thirty-five to forty birds present in Strybing as recently as 1997. In 1999 that number was down to between ten and twenty birds, with only two females among them. To try to reverse this trend, Strybing is planting shrubs which will provide food and shelter for them. These include native berries like thimbleberries and raspberries as well as native bunchgrass, California poppies, and other species which are good producers of seeds for the seed-loving quail.

The John Muir Trail is just one area in Strybing where California native plants are on display. The Redwood Nature Trail, to the east of the John Muir area, winds its way through a grove of California redwoods that are at least one hundred years old. Some of them were damaged in a huge wind storm which ravaged Golden Gate Park in 1995, but others remain. The forest understory receives more light these days, but it still is home to plants like native ginger and redwood sorrel.

Sisyrinchium bellum.
Blue-eyed grass is found in fields throughout California.
Margaret Armstrong, 1913.

Native California Garden

The star of the California collections is the Arthur L. Menzies Garden of California Native Plants. This hollow on the southern side of the garden is devoted to plants which thrive in California's warm, dry summers and mild winters.

When the winter rains come, the landscape is easy to appreciate. The flowers burst forth, the grasses turn green, and the catkins on the willows shudder provocatively in the breeze.

In the dry summer, however, the landscape may take getting to know in order to be properly appreciated. The sun beats down, and reflects upwards from the light-coloured soil. The predominant colors tend toward browns and dusty greens since many California plants go dormant during the dry season. Some trees even drop their leaves at the end of spring just as maples and oaks in colder climates drop theirs at the end of summer. Others have leaves which are hard and shiny, the better to conserve whatever moisture there is during the dry season.

At first encounter this landscape may seem harsh, even ugly. But once the visitor has taken the time to sit and savour the sights and smells the sparse beauty comes through. The elegant twists of the manzanita's dark red trunk, the seed pods hanging from the redbuds, the golden grasses growing out of the sandy soil, the dark green shade underneath the dome of a live oak: all are worth getting to know.

The Menzies Garden's explanations of relationships between plants, of how they have adapted to droughts, and the ways in which they were used by Native Americans are all interesting and clearly written. Mrs. Strybing, who was adamant that plants in the garden be labeled and wanted local plants included, would be pleased.

In the other areas where plants from Mediterranean-type climates grow, the explanations add much to the visitor's appreciation of what's to be seen. The fabulous protea flowers from South Africa, the Chilean ground covers now nearly ubiquitous in Southern California, the pungent eucalyptus from Australia—who would have guessed without the signs that they have evolved oceans away from each other to fill similar environmental niches.

The ancient geological connection of South Africa, Australia, and South America will also one day be made explicit. Hundreds of millions of years ago these land masses were part of an ancestral continent, which geologists have named Gondwanaland. Over the eons, the slow-working forces of plate tectonics rafted the lands apart, so that the only evidence of that early link is found today in the geologic record and in the similarities of certain plants. Medbury says that the plan is to put a granite sphere where Strybing's South African, Australian, and South American sections meet as a reminder of this ancestral link. (The sphere, he adds, will be very much like the one in the Singapore garden which is a monument to the Swiss Confederation.)

The one region which at the moment does not have its own sector is the Mediterranean. While plants from that region grow in several parts of the garden, like the Biblical Garden, there is no link among them. It is a lack which Medbury says the revised master plan hopes to remedy.

Medbury is optimistic that Strybing will be able to raise the necessary money to implement the changes without too much problem: "The Bay Area enjoyed a tremendous boom for a long time, and there is still a lot of money here." The funds raised may also be used to set up an endowment for maintenance and operating experiences. The current arrangement where about half Strybing's budget comes from San Francisco works well, he says, but the city is unable to commit itself to specific amounts for longer than a year at a time.

Two things must be considered when seeking outside financing. Charging admission fees to public services raises philosophical questions as well as the hard fact that a small admission fee may cost more to collect than it is worth. Also, when soliciting donations and gifts, considerable care has to be taken to avoid conflict of interests.

"One of the conditions of the Strybing bequest is that there be a medicinal garden," explains Medbury. "Up until now we have said that the Garden is full of medicinal plants, so that in a sense the entire Garden is a medicinal one. But there's one of the best medical schools right over there, just up the hill. A whole lot more could be done by involving it and pharmaceutical companies." The challenge is to set up terms of involvement to safeguard Strybing from adverse influences.

Strybing's future, though, is as bright as a March day after a rain. While it is not a large botanical garden, its research efforts are imaginative, its educational programs are dynamic, and its grounds are unique.

"We do not have enough land to make great contributions to plant genetic conservation," says Medbury. Doing that requires substantial space in order to hold multiple specimens of a plant of conservation concern, "but we can do great things in the area of conservation education."

Strybing already has a tradition of doing just that, of course: Peter Raven, director of the Missouri Botanical Garden and who grew up in San Francisco, was one of the young people whose enthusiasm for plants and nature was stimulated by botanizing and taking nature hikes at Strybing. Since then thousands of people, old and young, have taken courses offered by the Friends of the Garden, or visited the garden with a class, or spent a Sunday afternoon climbing in a tree house. In the future...well, in the future the San Francisco Bay Area, home of the original Silicon Valley, is likely to be one of the intellectual hotspots of the new century. Strybing could play a major role getting out the word about the importance of biodiversity and conservation.

To paraphrase the song from the 1960s: When you go to San Francisco, be sure to wear a flower in your hair. There's still no better place for flowers, or shrubs, or trees...

Protea cynaroides.
De Burggraaff *Sertum Botanicum*, 1828.

The University of British Columbia Botanical Garden
is set amid tall second-growth forest on Point Grey.
Photo by Mary Soderstrom.

A Garden on the Western Shore

THE UNIVERSITY OF BRITISH COLUMBIA Botanical Garden stands on the end of Point Grey, a promontory above the Strait of Georgia, that arm of the Pacific Ocean which separates Vancouver Island from the North American mainland. The garden in its present configuration is rather young, dating only from the 1960s, but because of its location and its design it closes a great circle that includes all the gardens visited in this book.

This is a place where great plates of the earth's crust collide, pushing up mountains and plunging down to form undersea abysses. The same sort of stresses are found in the San Francisco Bay area, but there the tension is causing parts of California to slip past each other. The Bay Area has high hills, to be sure, but not as many and as high, and certainly none rising precipitously behind the city like a painted backdrop the way Grouse Mountain rises behind Vancouver.

At the end of the UBC garden's entrance pavilion and from the edge of the lawn just outside the garden proper, the Strait and Vancouver Island can be seen through the trees. The Strait, in some places along its 200 km (124-mile) length, is as broad as a self-respecting sea while in others it is almost narrow enough to shout across. Here it is a good 70 km (more than 40 miles) wide. There are days when the vista is shrouded in fog or obscured by rain, but there are others when the sun sets riotously orange and red behind the distant hills.

When Captain George Vancouver sighted Point Grey in June 1792, it was covered by Douglas fir forest. "Gloomy" was the word he attached to it and to most of the scenery he saw as he and his crew explored the Strait of

Georgia. While many of his officers wrote with delight in their private journals of the "sublime" vistas of mountains, forest, and sea they encountered, Vancouver was not impressed. He had a job to do, which was to chart the area and reinforce Britain's claim on the Pacific coast. Spain and Britain had been quarreling over control, and a treaty in 1790 had decreed that ships from the two countries should map it.

He wasn't a stranger to the area. Nearly fifteen years earlier he had sailed on Captain James Cook's third voyage which had coasted along Vancouver Island, searching for a Pacific opening to a Northwest Passage between the Atlantic and the Pacific. Since then the Spanish had sent ships north from Mexico to lay claim to the coast. This was not the first time that the Spanish had explored the region. Two hundred years earlier a Greek pilot originally named Apostolos Valerianos but called Juan de Fuca by the Spanish for whom he was sailing, discovered the Strait which bears his name and which separates Vancouver Island from Washington's Olympic Peninsula, Canada from the U.S.

This time the Spanish ships were already anchored off Point Grey when Vancouver's men arrived. The two young captains of the Spanish ships, Dionisio Alcala Galiano and Cayetano Valdes, proceeded to explore the Strait with Vancouver's men, charting the inlets and narrows, and naming everything, frequently twice. While the names which Vancouver gave are the ones which show up most often on maps today, the connection with Spanish explorers live on with such names as Galiano Island, off the eastern coast of Vancouver Island, Valdez on the Alaska panhandle, and in Spanish Banks, on the northern flank of Point Grey.

This peaceful joint venture marked the end of an era. Spain would soon cede its claim to the territory to Britain. Thereafter the Spanish Empire would concentrate on the lands it already had colonized. Britain, which had just lost thirteen of its North American colonies, would nevertheless build an even larger empire. Plants from its far corners would fill the Royal Gardens at Kew, including many brought by Vancouver's expedition. The expedition's physician, Archibald Menzies, had been charged with plant collecting by Sir Joseph Banks, Kew's first director. Menzies complained in letters that Vancouver didn't take his collections seriously and that the goats and chickens on the ships ate some of them. Nevertheless, the monkey puzzle tree whose seeds he collected in Chile on the trip home caused a sensation when it was grown at Kew; its sharp-edged pyramidal leaves make

British Captain George Vancouver meeting Spanish Captain Francisco de la Bodega y Quadra. The mural, from a provincial government building in Victoria, B.C., reflects an early twentieth century view of native people. It commemorates the joint British-Spanish surveying of the British Columbia coast in 1792.
British Columbia Archives B-06670.

it impossible for even a monkey to climb, hence its name.

Cataloguing the plants of a region takes a long time, and, as we have seen, it is far from completed in the tropical world. In British Columbia the inventory was still going on more than a hundred years after Menzies began. Indeed cataloguing was one of the major reasons for setting up the antecedents of today's botanical garden. John Davidson, a largely self-educated, but first-class botanist from Scotland, arrived in Vancouver in April 1911 and in June was appointed the first provincial botanist. His mandate was to do a complete survey of British Columbia plants and to start a botanical garden and an herbarium of native plants. Davidson was allotted two acres on a farm east of Vancouver where, with the aid of ranchers, surveyors, teachers, and other volunteers, more than 700 species of native plants were established by 1914.

John Davidson on a field trip, ca. 1920.
In 1911 he was appointed the first provincial botanist.
British Columbia Archives.

That quick start ran into a setback two years later when the Provincial Botanical Office was abolished as part of the belt-tightening precipitated by World War I, which Canada, as part of the British Empire, entered in

1914, three years earlier than the United States. Responsibility for the herbarium and botanical garden were turned over to the fledgling University of British Columbia, even though the institution existed only in rented facilities and some dreams of a campus west of the city on Point Grey.

Davidson went ahead and arranged for the clearing and preparing of thirty-four hectares (eighty-five acres) of land on Point Grey. Then, like William Hammond Hall of San Francisco, he set about making the most of his site, although his task was much simpler than Hall's since he did not have to reclaim sand dunes. Davidson had the land drained and graded, and "green manured"—cropped successively with oats, rye and barley which were then plowed under. Most of the land became an experimental farm but two hectares (five acres) were set aside for the botanical garden. In little more than a year the collection, which now included 25,000 plants representing some 900 species, had been moved from the first site to Point Grey.

A good start, but practically nothing remains from this period today. The ups and downs of the garden's fortunes underline both the advantages and disadvantages to a botanical garden when it is part of another institution. Like the Jardin des Plantes in Paris which is part of the Muséum national d'Histoire naturelle, the UBC garden profits from the prestige and reputation of the larger institution, but on occasion it has found its interests subordinated to the priorities of others.

Throughout the 1920s both the UBC garden and the university grew rapidly. With the advent of the Great Depression in the 1930s, however, garden staff was cut drastically until there remained only two full-time employees and a boy hired part time to cut the lawns. This is in marked contrast to the gardens in San Francisco and Montreal, both independent organizations, which were able to take advantage of make-work programs during the Dirty Thirties.

Nevertheless, by the time Canada entered World War II in 1939, the UBC garden included medicinal beds, a rock garden, a willow collection, various display areas, an aquatic garden, beds planted according to groups of botanical categories, and an arboretum of native trees. This arrangement survived the war relatively unscathed.

When John Davdison retired in 1951, the garden found itself without its strongest advocate. Anyone who has visited the UBC Endowment lands has seen just how lovely the campus and its surroundings are. Given such natural beauty, it must not have seemed unreasonable to declare the entire campus a botanical garden in the 1950s. There followed more than ten years of campus growth during which it became clear that the garden and the need to provide parking for the expanding university were in deep conflict. It wasn't until 1968, when Roy Taylor took on the director's job and reported directly to the University's president, that today's gem of a garden had a chance to blossom.

The best approach to the campus from the center of Vancouver is along Northwest Marine Drive, past miles of beach bordering Spanish Banks. Across the water lies Vancouver's downtown, Stanley Park, and the mountains rising into the sky. Green College, where U.S. President Bill Clinton and the Soviet Union's Boris Yeltsin met in 1993 to officially end the Cold War, sits just inside the UBC campus, a wooded enclave filled with elegant architecture. Your first stop should be at Gate 4, to visit the Nitobe Memorial Garden.

A JAPANESE GARDEN

You are still three kilometers (1.86 miles) from the main botanical garden, but this informal Japanese stroll garden has been considered part of it since the little garden was ceremonially opened in 1960. It is dedicated to the memory of Dr. Inazo Nitobe, a Japanese educator, author, and diplomat who died in British Columbia's capital, Victoria, in 1933 on his way home from a peace conference in the Canadian Rockies. The University's president at the time had worked with Nitobe at the League of Nations after World War I. When Nitobe's friends commissioned a special Japanese lantern in his memory, it was brought from Japan and placed on the UBC campus. Ironically, this monument to a great proponent of peace was damaged during World War II by a vandal's gunshots. After the war, when the idea of a Japanese garden was suggested, the decision was made to name it after Nitobe, who has many memorials in Japan, including having his face on the Japanese 5,000 yen note.

Every feature in the garden is designed to reflect an idealized conception of nature with harmony among such natural forms as waterfalls, rivers, forests, islands, and seas. The path around the small lake at the center of the garden symbolizes the path through life with its good luck and bad fortune, its wise decisions and its disastrous ones. For most of the year, the palette of colours is predominately shades of green. In the spring, however, flowering cherries, azaleas, and iris contrast with the foliage, and in fall the maples turn shades of orange and scarlet. Koi, the goldfish-like Japanese Imperial carp, glide through the waters in the lake, a gift from the Jardin botanique de Montréal and its Japanese garden.

The Nitobe Memorial Garden is enclosed in a *tsujibei*, a traditional wall, which contributes to the garden's tranquillity. Nearby is UBC's Asian Centre whose landscaping flows seamlessly from the ancient traditions of the Nitobe garden, through modern interpretations of Asian gardening traditions, to the remnants of the Douglas fir forest which once covered the

A Japanese garden was created to honour the memory of
educator, author, and diplomat Dr. Inazo Nitobe.
Courtesy of UBC Botanical Garden.

area. While the Asian Centre has no formal connection with the botanical garden or the Nitobe garden, the mirror ponds, gravel arrangements, and carefully thought-out plantings show great sensitivity toward the philosophy underlying the Nitobe Garden.

Roy Taylor, who was chairman of the campus landscaping committee when the pavilion was being planned, says that construction plans for the Asian Centre originally called for cutting down many of the trees to provide parking. "We said that if that were done the Garden would have to be compensated for the loss, and when the value of the trees was factored in, it was decided to save them," he says now. "You can save trees but you have to make the effort to evaluate their worth."

Old growth trees of the British Columbia rain forest could be enormous.
This tree was felled near Vancouver in the late nineteenth century.
Photo by George Carey. British Columbia Archives, C-064-89.

And trees are the first things you notice when you enter the Botanical garden proper. A gorgeous stand of Douglas fir, western red cedar, grand fir, western hemlock, and other trees native to the region provide the backdrop for the administrative building and the Asian-inspired entrance. Some of the trees are as tall as 60 meters (200 feet) even though this is second growth. The site was logged in the 1870s, and only one 700-year-old Douglas fir remains from the original forest, but in Vancouver's wet climate trees grow relatively quickly. They provide the setting for the twelve-hectare (thirty-acre) David C. Lam Asian Garden, which is the first part of the Botanical Garden you encounter when you enter.

Like the Strybing garden in San Francisco, the UBC Botanical Garden has no display greenhouses. The first plan for the current site left room for classic desert and tropical glass house displays. It also had the entrance on the eastern side of Southwest Marine Drive, near the athletic stadium. But the glass house plans were shelved, and in a brilliant bit of re-jigging the entrance has been shifted across the road.

DAVID C. LAM ASIAN GARDEN
The change was financed by a $1 million gift from David Lam and his family. Lam, who served as British Columbia's Lieutenant Governor from 1988-94, and his wife Dorothy began attending home gardening classes

offered by the Garden in the 1970s and became very interested in the Garden's fortunes. Over the years they also became convinced that more should be made of the Garden's hundreds of plants from Asia. Their love of this unique collection resulted in their gift to the Garden.

The Asian collection began to be developed in 1976. The idea was to use the forest remnant as a framework to display plants which come from all over Asia and to take advantage of the site's special climatic patterns. Not only are strong northwest winds deflected up and over the site when they reach the ninety meter (300 foot) cliff on which the Lam garden stands, but also the dense forest moderates the temperature. Vancouver lies at the northern end of the dry summer, wet winter zone that begins in California. But the rains are harder—from 65 to 150 cm (26 to 60 inches). There is snow most years, up to 250 cm (100 inches), with an average of 55 cm (21 inches), and it is colder by far than San Francisco. This means that anything grown in much of Japan, in northern China, and in the higher altitudes of the Himalayas grows well in Vancouver.

The forest glades and open spaces provide a variety of microclimates for the many trees, shrubs, climbers, perennials, and ground covers which have been brought from Asia. In addition, for years the university's leaves and lawn clippings were composted at the edge of the woods. With this 'black gold" to enrich the soil, the plantings had the best possible start.

Today the Lam garden is a delight to all the senses. You enter by a boardwalk which extends out over a waterfall. The stream plunges into ponds where a variety of water-loving plants bloom from early spring to fall. Follow the sloping path which takes you closer to the water, or continue straight ahead past beds which are filled with lilies, azaleas, primulas, and other beauties depending on the season.

Along the winding paths 500 species of rhododendrons from Japan, Tibet, China, Korea, and Manchuria flower pink and red and scarlet. Nearly one hundred individual magnolias bloom beginning in February when the spearmint-scented *Magnolia sprengeri* Œ*Diva* blossoms.

Spring brings the spectacular flowering of the dove or handkerchief tree, *Davidia involucrata*, sent to France from China by Abbé Armand David in the 1860s. It gets its name from the three-inch long white bracts (not flowers) which flutter in the wind.

In fall, Asian varieties of mountain ash are laden with pink, white, yellow, or crimson fruits which are set off by the trees' airy foliage. Western dogwood, a native to coastal forests and British Columbia's official flower, and its Asian cousins also abound in the forest.

The Lam garden features several Stewartia, members of the tea family which are found in both the Eastern U.S. and in Asia. The plants at UBC are small ornamental trees with chestnut-coloured bark and green leaves which turn red and yellow in the fall. Through one of those quirky connections which often occur in the history of botanical gardens, they lead right back to Kew, and to George Vancouver's voyage. When Linnaeus was in the middle of his massive project of naming plants, he honoured

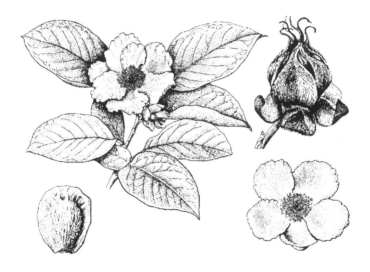

Stewartia ovata.

his friend, the amateur botanist John Stuart by naming a genus of the shrub after him, Stewartia. Bute's grandson, the Honourable Charles Stuart sailed with Vancouver as one of a group of well-bred teenaged underlings on his ship, and most certainly saw the original forest which covered Point Grey at that time.

Today, one of the grandest displays in the garden arrives in late spring when many of the vines are in bloom. To walk in the garden then is to be amazed at festoons of wisteria cascading from the tops of tree, and to be seduced by the flowers' perfume. There are benches in clearings where at any time of the year you can sit, listen to birds and admire the changing displays of Asian perennials. The native trees in the forest grow up to one hundred meters (330 feet) high, the light filters swimmingly to the understory, and the air is fragrant with the smell of cedar even when few flowers are in bloom. It is an breath-taking combination of nature and artifice, of native forest with plants from the other side of the Pacific. It looks natural in a way that is rare in botanical gardens.

BUDGET CUTS AND HUMAN CREATION

By following some of the paths to their end you will discover just how much a human creation the Lam garden is. At the extreme southern edge of the wood, signs warn that the paths further on are not maintained, and that budget constraints prevent the area being developed. Visitors are warned that they enter at their own risk. If you decide not to pay attention to the signs, you will soon see the difference between ordinary second-growth forest in this region and the Lam garden. The forest contains some beautiful trees, grown enormous in a rather short time, but the delightful details—the flowering ground cover, the vines climbing the trees, the rhododendrons bearing the last blossoms of the season—are not there. You will see dogwoods and a few other British Columbia natives, but missing is the carefully nurtured diversity and concentration of plants found in the Lam garden.

The posted signs and the undeveloped forest are two indications of the budget crunch the UBC garden has been forced to cope with for more than a decade. While adequate funding was available during the 1970s and early 1980s to get the rejuvenated botanical garden off to a great start, a combination of economic downturn and tight university funding translated into a series of budget cuts in the following years. Up to seven percent was shaved off the Garden's budget year after year from the mid-1980s until the turn of the century. When staff positions fell vacant they were not filled. The collections were merely maintained. The volunteer group, Friends of the Garden (FOGS), was called on to do much fund-raising, and brought in more than $1 million between 1992 and 2000. It took scrimping and creativity on the part of people like David Tarrant, education coordinator, to make what money there was go as far as possible. It is a great tribute to them that the visitor is not aware just how endangered the well-being of the garden was during this long period.

The future looks more promising. The current dean of the Faculty of

Asian traditions inspired the entrance pavillion to the
UBC Botanical Garden.
Photo by Mary Soderstrom.

Agricultural Sciences, Moura Quayle, is a landscape architect by training and a proponent of sustainable agriculture and biodiversity. The UBC Botanical Garden has a great role to play in the future, as part of an integrated, hybrid urban landscape, she says. With that official support, and with increased funding for higher education from the provincial and federal governments, the staff at the UBC garden is gearing up for new challenges.

The Garden has always worked closely with the local nursery industry to develop plants suited for the Pacific Northwest. This has given the Garden a platform for action during the long budget drought, says Douglas Justice, the newly-hired curator of collections. It also fulfills the Garden's mandate to produce plants which are well-adapted to the region, and to Canada.

Some of the most exciting plants developed at UBC are displayed in the theme gardens on the other side of Southwest Marine Drive. The busy road divides the Garden in half, but the Lam garden's designers cleverly solved the problem of how to get visitors from one side to the other by transforming a tunnel into a Moon Gate, which is completely in keeping with the Asian theme of the Lam garden.

BRILLIANT PERENNIALS

After passing through the gate-tunnel, you will find yourself out of the forest. Before you is a sloping passageway where brilliantly colored hardy plants are displayed on rocky walls on either side. Walk up the incline. At the top and to the left you will see the garden maintained by the volunteers, FOGS, to grow plants for arrangements and sales. Across from it is a perennial border, featuring plants chosen for their long periods of flowering and because they require little maintenance—an example for home gardeners as well as a joy to look at.

Like Kew, which is frequently rocked by noise from Heathrow International Airport, this portion of the UBC garden is invaded by sound. The only thing to do is concentrate on the sights and smells, and pretend that the sound of unseen traffic is that of the wind in the trees.

The Garden Pavilion, used for classes and special events, overlooks the several small gardens which make up the east side of the Botanical Garden. To the north lies a meadow, which in summer is home to a display of grasses and flowers which changes nearly daily as the season progresses. Stroll along the meadow, by the pond, and then swing east toward the Winter Garden. Vancouver has just about the mildest climate in Canada, and, despite the snow which falls most years, it is possible to have flowers all year here. Several varieties of heather provide masses of violet and mauve through much of the winter, while dark pink viburnum blooms from late October to February. Winter jasmine (*Jasminum nudiflorum*) flowers around Christmas-time. A number of plants with colourful berries or bright leaves provide contrast. Early varieties of bulbs like iris, crocus, scilla, and narcissus also flower shortly after the first of the year.

Just beyond the Winter Garden lies the E. H. Lohbrunner Alpine Garden. UBC's first alpine garden was laid out by John Davidson among some blocks left over from the building of the university's library. This new location is set on a slope, which provides good drainage, a necessity during Vancouver's long, wet winter since many alpine plants do not tolerate soggy soil. In addition, rock outcrops and different soil mixes have been provided to imitate the conditions that certain alpine plants require. The plants are grouped according to their geographical location. Every continent is represented, although only a few specimens are from the high, dry regions of Africa and Australia since most of those have great trouble in this much wetter climate.

NORTH AMERICAN PLANTS

Not surprisingly, the largest selection of plants in the Alpine Garden comes from North America. These include dwarf conifers and flowers which range from several varieties of three-petaled trillium to brightly colored penstemon. Bulbs from the mountains of Asia Minor—the home of tulips—brighten the garden in spring, while gentians from Asia provide masses of blue in late summer and early fall.

The B.C. Native Garden, right next to the Alpine Garden, was one of the first areas developed in this incarnation of the Botanical Garden. Begun in 1971 and formally opened in 1978, it provides several microclimates and ecological systems which are common in the province. The entry area features native plants which are good additions to home gardens, or which thrive when planted following road construction. A number of mature native trees—red cedar, hemlock, and Douglas fir—provide shade where plants like Oregon grape, trillium, and blue-and white camas lilies grow. Ferns, bog plants, wild ginger, and piggy bank plant (*Tolmiea menzeisii*) also grow well here. The latter plant, which is also used as a house plant, is named after Captain Vancouver's botanist Archibald Menzies.

One of the UBC Botanical Garden's major research undertakings has been cataloguing these native plants. Two editions of the *Flora of British Columbia* have been published with much assistance from the garden. Roy Taylor, director during the development of the modern garden, underscores the garden's "important work done in the promotion of the use of native plants in gardens." Native plants are better suited to local conditions, use less water, and are good for local birds and wildlife, he notes. A cooperative native plant instruction program, undertaken with the horticultural and garden industry, is a major way to "fulfill a botanical garden's role as steward of the plants in the local area as well as the steward-ship of the green earth as a whole."

The Food Garden, found west of the of BC Native garden and south of the Garden pavilion, showcases the kinds of fruits and vegetables that do well in the region. It is set off from the other gardens by a long arbour hung with climbing plants like wisteria, clematis, American bittersweet, and climbing hydrangeas and roses. On a hot afternoon it is tempting just to sit under the arbour, but the plants growing in the Food Garden deserve a close inspection. This section lies in a terraced hollow, so that the beds are exposed to the full sun, but are protected somewhat from the prevailing winds. Apples, pears, and cherries grow around the edge. Many are trained to grow on fences and in small compact shapes, demonstrating how fruit trees can thrive in spaces as confined as city backyards. The trees bear well, too, and the apple festival in the fall, put on by FOGS, is an annual crowd-pleaser.

SUSTAINABLE AGRICULTURE... AND COMMUNITIES

In the centre a wide variety of vegetables prosper. Beds overflowing with different kinds of pumpkin and squash plants produce luxuriant leaves and bright yellow flowers early in the summer, with the vegetables making

Oregon grape (Berberis repens)
Margaret Armstrong, 1913.

an inviting display themselves with the arrival of fall. Tomatoes, cabbages, broccoli...the list is long, and varies from year to year as the botanic garden experiments with new varieties to see how they fare in Vancouver's particular climate. FOGS, which helped research what to grow when the garden was first planted, continues to help with the harvesting and distribution of the garden's produce to the Salvation Army. It is fitting that the Food Garden is as lovely and productive as it is, because the UBC Faculty of Agricultural Sciences is deeply concerned about sustaining food production, healthy land, and communities in a proper balance. While the problems of monoculture are not present in British Columbia, farmers must be encouraged to be good stewards of the land, says Dean Quayle. Rewarding those who are is a goal of the Habitat Conservancy Trust and other organizations. But while the problems are global, solutions must be tailored to the specific conditions.

THE PHYSICK GARDEN: THE CIRCLE COMPLETES ITSELF
If you need proof that what that goes around, comes around, complete your visit to the UBC Botanical Garden with a walk through the Physick

Plants suitable to British Columbia are tested in the
Food Garden.
Photo by Mary Soderstrom.

Garden, which lies just behind an English yew hedge. The layout is inspired by a sixteenth century Dutch print of a monastery garden with twelve plots laid out around a sundial in the middle.

While the garden doesn't look like the Clusius Garden in Leiden, and its plants are the traditional ones used for medicine—valerian, chamomile, foxglove (digitalis),willow, bark and hollyhock and many others—there is no doubt that Clusius would find the garden familiar. It is even possible that some of the plants here may be direct descendants of ones which grew in Leiden. Allen Paterson, former director of the Chelsea Physick Garden, was involved in establishing UBC's physick garden, and contributed thirty-seven packets of seeds from the English garden. "Who knows?" asks David Tarrant. "The Chelsea garden exchanged plants with other gardens in Europe, so there is likely a link between our garden and all the other early botanical gardens."

Wheels within wheels. One of the things that humans like to do is look for patterns, and there are plenty here. From Leiden University to the University of British Columbia, from the sixteenth century to the twenty-first, botanical gardens provide a link just as they provide pleasure and the means to understand and perhaps safeguard the natural world.

That is why, says UBC's Dean Quayle, in the future they could become integral parts of a web of nature extending throughout the community, linking other gardens, parks and greenways.

Gardens of the Future

IN THE BEGINNING was the garden...

There is no question that people love all kinds of gardens. Each year we spend billions on flowers, plants and garden supplies, and we flock to visit botanical and other kinds of gardens by the millions. The desire to make new botanical gardens is still with us. In the United Kingdom two have just opened their gates for the first time, the Eden Project in Cornwall and the National Botanical Garden of Wales. There also are plans for new ones in Russia, in Connecticut, in Tuscany, not to mention Strybing's plans to rethink and rework its already remarkable garden.

What is in question, however, is the form which botanical gardens will take in a world with six, eight or ten billion people. Will they become merely theme parks for plants, competing with multiplex cinemas and inter-active video for recreation dollars? Or will they continue not only to delight, but also to make a difference in how the world rolls on?

Over the last three years I have visited all the gardens I write about here. They are beautiful, every one, and I delighted in the time I spent in them. In addition, despite their varying size, history and emphasis, I have found several family resemblances among them which say much about the way ideas travel from one part of the world to the other, about things people have in common, and about our dependence on the natural world.

An example is the way the main gate into the Singapore Botanic Garden is a less elaborate model of the Decimus Burton's gate at Kew. It is not far fetched to view that gate as a concrete symbol of how Kew opened the way to the establishment of gardens and botanical research in the British Empire's colonies. Consciously or unconsciously, the gates that Henry Shaw designed for his mausoleum garden also declare his and the Missouri Botanical Garden's roots in the tradition of British gardens and the formidable intellectual heritage of Kew.

Another resemblance is the way the grand view from the Monterey Cypress at Strybing in San Francisco echoes the vista from the steps of the Palm House at Kew toward the ancient Cedar of Lebanon. Then there are the Moon Gate in the Margaret Grigg Nanjing Friendship Garden at the Missouri Botanical Garden, the Moon Gate leading from one side of the UBC Botanical Garden to the other, as well as one in Dream Lake Garden of the Jardin botanique in Montreal. The elegant patterns of raked gravel in the Japanese gardens at Leiden, in St. Louis, and at Kew all also refer to similar influences. Not to mention features which might be found on a checklist of what to put in an interesting botanical garden: rose gardens, alpine gardens, Linnaean or systematic gardens, medicinal or physick gardens, parterres brilliant with tulips or annuals, and stands of flowering shrubs, be they lilacs, camellias, the orchid Vanda Miss Joaquim or something else, depending on the garden's climate.

There are other resemblances which fall outside conscious garden planning. Chief among them are the way each garden nurtures expanses of lawn, no matter how difficult it may be to grow grass. In Singapore, garden officials despaired about the way the lawn looked: "We do not have the equipment, the garden workers are not trained, the lawns just do not look the way they should." The lawns looked pretty good to me.

In San Francisco, where it rains only in winter and the lawns are watered sparingly from wells in the garden, the grass is nevertheless coaxed into growing year round. Even in Missouri where Henry Shaw chose the botanical garden's site because of its beautiful prairie, growing grass is not a simple thing. At the Shaw Arboretum where farmland has lain fallow for sixty or seventy years, trees are steadily encroaching on the meadows. Nevertheless, the lawns are there, and almost everyone loves them. Similarly, every garden has at least a few big trees which are particularly prized: Strybing's Monterey Cypress, the Jardin des Plantes' Chinese Pagoda tree, and Singapore's Palm Valley are examples. The chestnuts and maples at Leiden even survived the Hunger Winter of 1944-45, despite the terrible shortage of fuel.

All this speaks to a universal desire to situate ourselves in good, green places, just as our ancestors over the eons chose places that promised food to gather, water to drink and good forage for animals they wanted to hunt. Sadly, however, some features of modern life which degrade the planet have their origins in this quest for good places to live. Take our romance in North America and parts of Europe with single-family houses, quarter-acre lots, and suburban sprawl. The result may mean a little patch of green to call your own, but building houses in bucolic settings also entails massive habitat destruction. What is worse, getting to these houses usually means travel by automobile, with the resulting air pollution and production of greenhouse gases.

Those are just the close-to-home effects of the way we in the developed world live. Our standard of living has much wider repercussions: the rubber for the tires comes from the tropics, aluminum and iron ore come from other fragile zones, the tankers that ship the oil used to make gasoline travel dangerous sea routes. It is a terrible irony that in trying to find the surroundings that we naturally prefer, we in the developed world are destroying nature.

The rest of the world does not live like this, and it is not clear if it ever will. Peter Raven of the Missouri Botanical Garden likes to tell a story about Mahatma Gandhi. When India gained its independence in 1947, Ghandi was asked if he thought his country would be able to provide its citizens with the same standard of living that existed in Britain. Ghandhi replied that since it took half the world to support the standard for the forty million people in Britain, doing so for 400 million in India would surpass the resources of the planet. That, says Raven, is one of the truths that we all are going to have to come to terms with.

Stop! I know what is coming next, the reader who has made it this far may think. She is going to embark on a long diatribe about how the world is going to hell in a handcart, and that is not what I bargained for when I began reading this book about gardens.

I can understand that reaction. Looking at pictures of gardens and reading about their splendours are much more pleasant than having the world's problems forced on you. Who wants to hear about the destruction of the rain forest, or the way that sewage and run-off from agriculture have created at least fifty dead zones in the world's seas? Or about global warming and crops failing because climate change brings drought or flooding, or about malaria surging back because mosquitoes find more places to breed in deforested land? About mass migrations of people toward cities where they think things might be better? About the civil unrest which often follows when urban life turns out to be worse?

But bear with me a bit longer. I'm not alone in enticing people with the beauty of nature, and then moving on to less pleasant territory. The message of conservation, of the importance of safeguarding this planet, is the subtext of nearly every exhibit in most gardens today.

There is another reason for your forbearance: I want to talk about hope, and how people can make a difference, particularly if they are aware of what is at stake and of the contradictions between what we love and the destruction we often wreak to get it.

The first botanical gardens were supported by beliefs which simply are not widely held any more. Where many early botanists believed it might be literally possible to recreate Eden, and later ones studied God in the beauty of the plants they believed he created, most of today's scientists do not believe in God. (No more than forty percent, according to a survey which was the subject of an article in *Scientific American* in 1999.) Nevertheless, nearly all the scientists I encountered when working on this book described their involvement in spiritual terms, whether or not they were traditional believers. They used the word "biodiversity" as often and with as much reverence as their predecessors said "God."

Some, like Raven of the Missouri Botanical Garden, think that this respect for the natural world may turn out to be the source of a movement which will eventually convince us all to make the changes necessary to truly safeguard nature. It may take someone of the stature of a Gandhi, St. Francis, or Martin Luther King to inspire people to act decisively, Raven says, but in the meantime, leaders, philosophers, and religious people can be enlisted to help. Stewardship of our planet should be a goal for all of us.

And there is some good news from the front, too. Things have actually improved some places. In the United Kingdom and North America, we no longer have to contend with pollution from coal-fueled industry which was so bad at one point that the Missouri Botanical Garden considered moving out of St. Louis ,and plants in the greenhouses at Kew did not get enough light. The Asian garden at Vancouver's UBC garden also demonstrates that, given proper care and respect, a second growth forest filled with sylvan giants can still grow. And the gingko, that lovely Chinese tree, thrives around the world even though in the seventeenth century it appeared

Ginkgo, *Flora Japonica*. Siebold and Zuccarini.

extinct in the wild and was found only in a few monastery gardens.

These are skirmishes in the larger battle. Thinking about them should give us courage to look for larger solutions, and to make careful choices in our own lives. What fertilizers and pesticides do we put on our own gardens? Where does the food we eat come from? Is this car trip necessary? And, come election time, does that politician realize the global implications of this international treaty and that financial arrangement?

Garden lovers should also insist that botanical gardens be financed by all of us, largely through our taxes. Botanical gardens must continue to catalogue and safeguard the earth's wealth of plants and to lay the ground work through conservation education for larger changes required to sustain this green earth. They must not waste their energies trying to fill the budget gaps left when governments decide to cut back. They should be beautiful and interesting, attracting people of every age from every part of society, but they should not have to compete head to head with amusement parks for income from admissions in order to survive. And, perhaps especially, they should not be left vulnerable to influence by whatever organization or individual pays the bills.

These are relatively small things that can make big differences, but gardeners, perhaps more than anyone else, understand that small actions today will have major effects tomorrow.

As I write this, two tall gingkos, male and female, grow not far from where I sit. These are not trees cosseted by dedicated crews in a botanical garden, but ones planted seventy or eighty years ago in a private garden which has since become a pleasant but rather ordinary city park. The trees are not unique. There are millions of them today.

When I finish, I will go for a walk in the first snow of the season, an unusually early snow in a year of crazy weather. The gingkos, in their fall dress, will be glowing brilliant yellow. I will pause in the last light of a dark autumn day and remember with thanks the Chinese Emperor Shen Nung who collected the trees 3,000 years ago, the monks who preserved them in monastery gardens over the centuries, Engelbert Kaempfer who brought their seeds back to Holland, and the botanists who ensured that they were spread to the four corners of the globe. Their individual actions made a difference, as can ours.

In the beginning was the garden ... and with luck and hard work we can assure that there always will be.

The Gardens at a Glance

Hortus Botanicus of the University of Leiden, Holland
Rapenburg 73, Leiden

Mailing address: P.O. Box 9516, 2300 RA, Leiden
Telephone: 071-5277249
Website: http://www.hortus.leidenuniv.nl/
Entrance fee: Florins 8

Hours
March 25 to October 27: Daily from 10 to 18:00 hours (6 p.m.); From October 28 to March 24, 10 to 16:00 (4 p.m.) The entire garden is closed on February 8, October 3, and December 24 to January 1.

Size: 2.6 hectares (6.4 acres)
Date founded: 1590

How to get there
Holland has excellent rail transportation, so wherever you are staying take the train to Leiden. From there walk or take a taxi along the canals (about a ten-minute walk). There's a large map in the big square just outside the train station where you can get your bearings.

What to look for in particular
The Clusius Garden is a reproduction of the original botanical garden, designed by the botanist Clusius in 1590. In high summer it is lovely.

Other nearby gardens worth visiting
The De Keukenhof Park is 70 hectares (175 acres) filled with millions of tulips and other bulb flowers in April and May. Located at Lisse between Leiden and Haarlem. Inquire at train stations about the frequent rail service.

Le Jardin des Plantes of the Muséum national d'Histoire naturelle
57, rue Cuvier, Paris V^e

Telephone: 01 40 79 30 00
Website: http://www.mnhn.fr/expo/lieuxMNHN/TextesFrancais/PagesLieux/jplant.html
Entrance fees: Free for the main Jardin. Small entrance fees for the Jardin alpin and the glass houses, and for exhibits in the Grande Galerie de l'Evolution.

Hours
7: 30 to 17: 30 (5:30 p.m.) in the winter, and until 20:00 (8 p.m.) in the summer.

Size: 22 hectares (67 acres)
Date founded: 1635 by edict of Louis XIII

How to get there
Metro Censier-Daubenton, and then follow the signs east. Or Gare d'Austerlitz, and walk west. The gates are opposite the Pont d'Austerlitz.

What to look for in particular
This is a garden which Paris has grown up around. Specimen trees: a black locust dating back to 1625, a gem of an alpine garden, glass houses which inspired Henri Rousseau to paint his jungle scenes. Interesting exhibits and lectures about natural science in the Grand Galerie de l'Évolution.

Other nearby gardens worth visiting
In the immediate vicinity is the Jardin de Luxembourg, formal gardens around the Palais de Luxembourg, built by Henri IV for his queen Marie de Medici (Metro Luxembourg). Also Jardin Tino Rossi, a sculpture garden along the Seine downstream from the Pont Austerlitz which offers grand views of the river, as well as lovely rhododendrons in May. The Musée de Cluny (corner of Boulevard Saint-Michel and Boulevard Saint-Germain) has also recently opened a medieval garden.

And don't miss the Arboretum national de Chèvreloup in Versailles. A good day trip is to visit the gardens at Versailles in the morning, and then spend the afternoon in the Arboretum. The contrast is striking: one is crowded and very formal, the other is nearly deserted and very much a nature refuge. From the Versailles train stations take the B or H bus to the stop at the Parly II shopping centre. Don't be put off by the un-garden-like surroundings, but get off and walk past the shopping centre. On the other side you will find an underpass leading to the arboretum.

~·ఴ·~

The Royal Botanic Gardens at Kew
Kew, Surrey, Richmond

Telephone: +44 (0) 20 8940 1171 (24-hour service for opening hours, etc.)
Website: http://www.rbgkew.org.uk/
Entrance fees: Adults, £5.50, age sixteen and under, free; senior citizens, full-time students, the unemployed and those on income assistance programs, £4.50; Children between 5 and 16, £2.50; Family, £13. In addition there are special rates for season tickets.

Hours: Open at 9:30 a.m. daily, with varying closing times depending on the season (4:15 p.m. in winter to 7:30 p.m. on summer weekends). Closed Christmas Day and New Year's Day.

Size: 180 hectares (440 acres)

Date founded
Usually counted from the time when Frederick and Augusta, the Prince and Princess of Wales, began developing the garden in 1759. It had a second birth in 1844, however, when it became separately funded and run.

How to get there
The Silverlink or District Line to Kew Gardens Station, with a five minute walk through the charming village of Kew is probably the easiest. The website has detailed bus and car directions, and there is boat service up the Thames from Westminster. Arrivals and departures aren't frequent but you can imagine that you're a royal courtier, coming up to enjoy country life.

What to look for in particular
Where to start? Kew is magnificent and worth a day or more if you have the time. The Palm House, Princess of Wales Conservatory, and Temperate House are outstanding greenhouses, while the grounds are simply beautiful. Start walking, and whatever you see will be amazing.

Other nearby gardens worth visiting
Wakehurst Place is Kew's sister garden. It is not as easy to get to, but offers several different habitats and an Elizabethan mansion. Tel: 01444 894066. Haywards Heath is the nearest train, then it's six miles by taxi or bus (82, and 88 on Sundays and Bank Holidays.) In London, the Chelsea Physick Garden still exists, and is open on Wednesday and Saturday afternoons. The city is full of parks with grand horticultural displays. Tulips in Embankment Park or Holland Park are gorgeous in May, for example.

The Singapore Botanic Gardens
1 Cluny Road
Singapore 259569

Telephone: 4719943
Website: http://www.nparks.gov.sg/sbg
Entrance fees: Admission to the garden is free. The National Orchid Garden: $S2. for adults, $S1 for children.
Hours: open daily from 5 a.m. to midnight.

Size: 47.4 hectares (117 acres)

Date founded
1859 as part of the network of colonial botanical gardens, loosely linked to the Royal Botanic Gardens at Kew. All Southeast Asia's rubber plantations are descended from eleven rubber plants acclimatized here. It currently is deeply involved in taxonomy.

How to get there

You can get direct flights to Singapore from the West Coast on several airlines, or by way of other major Asian cities. Or go the other way round: Air France has flights from Paris and since you are allowed one stop-over you could visit the Jardin des Plantes on the same trip. Once you arrive, you'll find Singapore's public transportation system is excellent, and it's worth buying the little Transitlink Guide for $2 to help you get around. The botanical gardens can be reached by taking several buses, among them the 7, 77, 106, 123 and 174 buses from the Orchard MRT station.

What to look for in particular

The palm trees, the orchids, the anthuriums: everything that you ever grew as a house plant is here but three times as big. Singapore is a rich, jazzy, safe bit of Asia. From the time you leave the airport, you're surrounded by flowers and greenery, the result of more than thirty years of Green City policy. Consider visiting the botanic gardens early in the morning, late afternoon or early evening; at midday it's so hot you'll want to retreat to air-conditioning or sit under a fan.

Other nearby gardens worth visiting

Bukit Timah Nature Reserve, featuring original jungle, covers the top of Singapore's highest hill. Take the 67 bus from the Newton MRT station. The Chinese and Japanese Gardens on the western end of the island are commercial gardens well worth seeing. Take the MRT to the Chinese Garden Station. The Manda Orchid Gardens are a nursery which grows nothing but orchids. Take the 137 bus from Ang Mo Kio MRT station.

The Missouri Botanical Garden
4344 Shaw Boulevard

Mailing address: P.O. Box 299, St. Louis MO 63166-0199
Telephone: (314) 577-5100
Website: http://www.mobot.org/welcome.html
Entrance fees
The Missouri Botanical Garden is free for members of the Garden, while residents of St. Louis get a discount. For visitors age 13 to 64, admission is $7, seniors age 65 or more it is $5 and children 12 and under are free. Admission to the Tower Grove House is free to members and children under six, $3.00 for adults, and $.50 for children between the ages of 6 and 12. Narrated tram rides are $3.00 for adults and free for children under six.
Note: Some special events may require an additional charge.

Hours
9 a.m. to 5 p.m. daily, except for Mondays from Memorial Day to Labour Day when the garden is open until 8:00 p.m. Wednesdays and Saturdays the grounds are open for walking from 7-9 a.m. Closed Christmas Day.

Size: 31.6 hectares (79 acres)

Date founded
1859 by a Henry Shaw, an Englishman who made his fortune in the frontier town of St. Louis, and then, influenced by the great Victorian gardens, decided to make a botanical garden for his fellow citizens.

How to get there
The Missouri Botanical Garden is accessible via public transportation by taking the MetroLink to the Central West End station and catching the Garden Express shuttle bus. When coming by car, watch for the exit signs off Interstate 44.

What to look for in particular
This garden mixes many small garden areas with pieces of sculpture and fountains. Since St. Louis can be very hot, the water features are particularly lovely. The Japanese and Chinese gardens are authentic and beautiful, while the many other features educate and amuse.

Other nearby gardens worth visiting
Shaw Arboretum 35 miles southwest of St. Louis in Gray Summit, Missouri, at the intersections of Hwy. 100 and Interstate 44. St. Louis has two large parks with fine gardens, Tower Grove Park and Forest Park. St. Charles, 30 minutes by highway west of St. Louis, is the state's first capital, and the place where the Louis and Clark expedition started out. You can near the un-flood-controlled Missouri river there too.

The New York Botanical Garden
200th St. and Kazimiroff Boulevard
Bronx, New York, N.Y. 10458

Telephone: (718) 817-8700
Website: http://www.nybg.org/
Entrance fees
The Garden grounds admission is $3 for adults; $2 for senior citizens and students; $1 for children 2-12. Separate fees for the tram ride, Everett Children's Adventure Garden, Enid A. Haupt Conservatory, Rock Garden, and Native Plant Garden. The Narrated Tram Tour Garden Passport which includes all the above is $10 for adults, $7.50 for seniors and students, and $4 for children ages two to 12.

Hours:
The Garden is open all year. 10 a.m. to 6 p.m. (April - October), 10 a.m. to 4 p.m. (November - March) Tuesday - Sunday and Monday Holidays. Closed Mondays, Thanksgiving, and Christmas Day.

Size: 100 hectares (250 acres)

Date founded
1891, with the sponsorship of New York's movers and shakers. Support from them has continued throughout its history.

223

How to get there

The Garden is easy to reach by public transportation: 20 minutes from midtown, 20 minutes from central Westchester, 10 minutes from major bridges, and 20 minutes from Grand Central Terminal via Metro-North Railroad to the Garden's Main Gate. When coming by car on the Major Deegan Expressway, look for NYBG signs at the 200 St. exit.

What to look for in particular

The Enid A. Haupt Conservatory is a lovely Victorian glass house filled with plants from ecosystems around the world. The hemlock forest at the center of the garden is unique, and a hint of what New York was like before Europeans arrived. But the garden contains 48 separate gardens and collections which would be difficult to see in one visit. Perhaps the best strategy is to look carefully at the brochure handed out when you enter. It suggests circle tours, based on what part of the garden is at its best that particular season.

Other nearby gardens worth visiting

The Cloisters, part of the Metropolitan Museum of Art, sits on the tip of Manhattan. It incorporates elements of five medieval French cloisters with 5,000 works of art from the period, and medieval gardens. The Brooklyn Botanical Garden, is a smaller, young botanical garden, but worth a visit. http://www.bbg.org/

Jardin botanique de Montréal
4101, rue Sherbrooke Est
Montréal QC H1X 2H2

Telephone: (514) 872-1400
Website: http://www.ville.montreal.qc.ca/jardin/jardin.htm
Entrance fees
Jardin and Insectarium, from April 28 to Nov. 4: adults, $10.00; age 65 and older, and students $7.50; age six to 17, $5. The rest of the year: adults, $7.25; age 65 and older, and students, $5.75; age six to 17, $3.75. The summer time tram tour is free. Special rates are available for the Jardin, Insectarium, and Biodôme. Discounts are given to Montreal residents with the Accès Montréal card.

Hours: Nov. 1 to June 15, 9 a.m. to 5 p.m.; from June 16 to September 12, 9 a.m. to 7 p.m.; from September 13 to October 31,9 a.m. to 9 p.m. Open every day of the year.

Size: 75 hectares (185 acres)

Date founded
1939. Brother Marie-Victorin, a cleric/botanist and Henry Teuscher, a landscape architect trained in Europe and the United States, had been planning a botanical garden for years. They were able to use the make-work projects of the 1930s to

construct the garden. Since then it has become one of the largest and best in the world.

How to get there

Get off at the Pie IX Metro station and walk up the hill or catch the 139 Bus (keep your Metro transfer). Or take the 185 bus on Sherbrooke East When going by car, find Sherbrooke Street, the longest street on the island of Montreal. If you drive along its eastern section you will eventually reach the Jardin. Need a landmark on the skyline to orient yourself? The tower of the Olympic Stadium is nearby.

What to look for in particular

This is another big garden, so taking the tram ride (free in summer) will give you a good overview of the Jardin. But if you want just a quick look around, hit the exposition and economic gardens just north of the restaurant, swing through the Alpine Garden, make a quick visit to the Chinese and Japanese gardens, and conclude your visit with a look at the greenhouses.

Other nearby gardens worth visiting

The Morgan Arboretum in Sainte-Anne-de-Bellevue on the western tip of Montreal Island is worth a trip. In summer, Montreal also has many horticultural displays in parks and on the median strips of boulevards, which are the legacy of a mayor who was director of the Jardin. For trips further afield, Old Field Garden (http://www.oldfieldgarden.on.ca/) in Alexandria, Ontario, two hours west of Montreal, and the Jardin de Métis (http://www.jardinsmetis.com/), six hours east of Montreal on the south shore of the St. Lawrence.

Strybing Arboretum and Botanical Gardens
9th Avenue at Lincoln Way
Golden Gate Park
San Francisco CA 94122

Telephone (415) 661-1316
Website: http://www.strybing.org/
Entrance Fee: Free

Hours

Open every day of the year. Weekdays: 8 a.m. to 4:30 p.m. Weekends and holidays 10 a.m. to 5 p.m.. Free guided tours daily at 1:30 p.m., on weekends at 10:00 a.m. and 1:30 p.m.

Size: 22 hectares (55 acres)

Date founded

Opened in 1940 in Golden Gate Park, but many trees had already been planted since an arboretum and botanic garden had been desired since the 1870s.

How to get there
Lincoln Way crosses US Highway 1 about a half mile west of Strybing. Strybing is served by several bus and streetcar lines. Call (415) 673-MUNI for information.

What to look for in particular
In this garden without greenhouses, plants from Mediterranean climates are the standout feature. Check out the South African, Chilean, and Australian sectors, as well as the Cloud forests, both Southeast Asian and Meso-American. The Arthur L. Menzies Garden of California Native Plants has great explanatory materials, and is unlike what you will find in other botanical gardens. The Garden of Primitive Plants also is unique.

Other nearby gardens worth visiting
Across the Bay, the University of California at Berkeley has a 14 hectare (35 acre) botanical garden in the hills behind the campus.
http://www.mip.berkeley.edu/garden/
     Also interesting in spring are the Rhododendron Dell in Golden Gate Park and the Berkeley Rose Garden.

The University of British Columbia Botanical Garden
6804 S.W. Marine Drive
Vancouver, B.C. V6T 1Z4

Telephone: (604) 823-9666
Website: http://www.hedgerows.com/UBCBotGdn/
Entrance fees
Adults: $4.75 ($6 including the Nitobe Gardens); Student (Grades 1 to 7), $2; student (high school, community college, university) $2.50; age 65 and older, $2.50; UBC student with card, free; children under 6, free

Hours: Spring/Summer hours: 10:00 a.m. to 6:00 p.m. daily. From October 9 to March 15: 10 a.m. to 2:30 p.m. The Nitobe Garden is not open weekends in winter.

Size: 21 hectares (51.5 acres)

Date founded: 1912, but current garden begun in 1968.

How to get there: The Spanish Banks # 42 Bus will get you there. By car, you can take 16th Avenue to Marine Drive. The gardens are located on the corner. From the South, take Southwest Marine Drive once you cross the Oak Street Bridge. The most scenic route is from the north along West Marine Drive.

What to look for in particular
Be sure to stop at the Nitobe Memorial Japanese Garden before you get to the botanical garden proper. Once there you won't be able to miss the David C. Lam Asian Garden which is simply splendid. Also interesting are the Food Garden, the Physick Garden, and the many displays of perennials.

Other nearby gardens worth visiting
The Sun Yat Sen Garden in downtown Vancouver, and the VanDusen Botanic Gardens about 5 kilometers east of UBC. See the website: http://www.city.vancouver.bc.ca/parks/parks&gardens/vandusen/default.shtml

Sources

This book is meant to be a pleasure to read, both at home and when visiting gardens. Therefore I decided not to footnote the sources throughout the text, because that would break both the narrative of history and the charm of a garden stroll. But I consulted many sources and interviewed many people while writing it. My thanks to all those who helped me are found in a separate note. What you'll find below is a bibliographic summary which includes not only books and other printed documents, but also references to some websites, personal communications, and interviews.

In the Beginning ...
There are three books which started me thinking about botanical gardens. I am much indebted to John Prest's *The Garden of Eden: The Botanic Garden and the Re-Creation of Paradise* (Yale University Press: New Haven and London, 1981) for demonstrating how almost absolute was the belief in the literal existence of the Garden of Eden, and how that belief changed under the onslaught of the New World's wealth of hitherto unknown plants. Also useful was *The Discoverers: A History of Man's Search to Know His World and Himself* by Daniel J. Boorstin (Random House: New York and Toronto, 1983), particularly the section "The Geography of the Imagination." Few histories of gardens or botany consider the structure of commonly held beliefs during the late Middle Ages and Renaissance. *Great Botanical Gardens of the World* by Edward Hyams, with photographs by William Macquitty, (Bloomsbury Books: London,1969) introduced me to many gardens I had never heard of, and helped me choose the nine I write about here.

As for the evolutionary psychology approach to landscape, the best introductory essay remains "Evolved Responses to Landscape" by Gordon H. Orians and Judith Heerwagen in *The Adapted Mind* , ed. by Jerome H. Barkow, Leda Cosmides, and John Tooby (Oxford University Press: New York and Oxford, 1992).

The Garden of the Dutch Empire: Leiden
Two books were particularly useful in writing this chapter: *1587-1937 Hortus Academicus Lugduno Batavus: The Development of the Gardens of Leyden* and *The Authentic Garden: A Symposium on Gardens* edited by L. Tjon Sie Fat and E. de Jong, (Clusius Foundation: Leiden, Netherlands, 1991). The former book I found in the Library of the Jardin botanique de Montréal; it had been part of the private library of the Jardin's designer, Henry Teuscher, which was willed to the Jardin's library at his death. The other book is in the collection of the Canadian Centre for Architecture. The guide to the Hortus Botanicus was also interesting, useful, and a great way to relive my afternoon in the garden. Figures for language distributions are from *Ethnologue,* 13th edition 1999.

Also useful was the website of the Deshima Island restoration project: http://www1.city.nagasaki.nagasaki.jp/dejima/index_e.htmll, as was the Unversity of Uppsala's web site— http://www.systbot.uu.se/dept/history/linneaus.html, which provides references and much informaton about Carolus Linnaeus. Jan de Koning, Gerda van Uffelen, and Constanze van der Veen of the Hortus Botanicus answered my many questions promptly and with great good humour. Ms. van der Veen also provided archival photographs.

The Garden of the French Empire: Le Jardin des Plantes, Paris

There is little available in English about the Jardin des plantes, but *Le Muséum national d'Histoire naturelle*, by Yves Laissus, in the Découvertes Gallimard series (Paris, 1995) gives a complete and well-illustrated overview. Also interesting is the biography *Buffon*, by Jacques Roger, (Fayard, 1989), as is *Paris Deux mille ans d'histoire* by Jean Favier (Fayard, 1997).

For further information I am endebted to Yves-Marie Allain, director of the Jardin's Service des cultures. Not only did he answer my questions at length and provide several articles and Muséum publications, he saw that I had a copy of the 1997 "Etude préalable à la mise en valeur du Jardin des Plantes de Paris" by Marion Bosser, Valérie Gaudin, Yasmine Sentissi, and Hélène Sirieys, under the direction of Janine Christiany.

Among the many interesting and useful publications of the Muséum, I consulted *Le Jardin alpin du Jardin des Plantes de Paris*, by Michel Flandrin (2000), *Les arbres historiques du Jardin des Plantes*, by Maïté Delmas-Trolliet (1993), *Le Tour du monde en 800 arbres, Visite guidée de l'Arboretum national de Chèvreloup* (1991), *Le Jardin alpin du Jardin des Plantes* by Sovanmoly Hul et Michel Jakubyszyn (1990), *Les Grandes serres du Jardin des Plantes* by Y. Delange (1988), and *Les herbes folles du Jardin des Plantes* by Paul Jovet et Bernadette Lizet (1988) Equally interesting were two articles: "Promenade au Jardin des Plantes" by Jérome Coignard *Beaux Arts Magazine*, juillet, 1997 and "Le Jardin" by Yves-Marie Allain, *Conaissance des arts* (Numéro hors-série 1995).

In addition several entries in *The New Catholic Encyclopedia* provided information about French missionary/botanists; the web site is at: http://www.newadvent.org/cathen/

The Ralph Waldo Emerson quote is from "The Uses of Natural History," published in *The Early Lectures of Ralph Waldo Emerson*, ed. Stephen Whicher and George Spiller (Cambridge, Mass., 1959).

The Garden of the British Empire: The Royal Botanic Gardens at Kew

There's a wealth of information available about the Royal Botanic Gardens at Kew. The following books were particularly helpful: David Blomfield, *The Story of Kew* (Second Edition, Leyborne Publications: Kew, 1992); Wilfrid Blunt, *In for Penny: A Prospect of Kew Gardens: Their Flora, Fauna and Falballas* (Hamish Hamiton in Association with the Tyron Gallery: London, 1978); Lucile H. Brockway, *Science and Colonial Expansion: The Role of the British Royal Botanic Gardens* (Academic Press New York: London, 1979); F. Nigel Hepper, editor *Royal Botanic Gardens Kew, Gardens for Science and Pleasure* (Her Majesty's Stationery Office: London, 1982); F. Nigel Hepper, editor of *Plant Hunting for Kew*, (Her Majesty's Stationery Office: London, 1989); Clive Langmead, *A Passion for Plants: The Life and Vision of Ghillean Prance* (Lion Publishing: Oxford, 1995); Donal P. McCracken, *Gardens of Empire: Botanical Institutions of the*

Victorian British Empire (Leicester University Press: London and Herndon, VA, 1997.) In addition the quarterly publication of the Friends of Kew, *Kew* and *Kew Scientist* were extremely interesting and helpful. Peter Crane, the current director, answered my many questions.

A Gem of a Garden in the Tropics: Singapore

Singapore is one of the most wired places in the world, and when looking for background information, I found netsurfing rewarding. Among the finds were Darren Tan's fascinating paper on housing in Singapore done for the University of New South Wales, http://www.fbe.unsw.edu.au/research/student/SgPubHous/ For information about Singapore's continued strategic position see: John H. Noer and David Gregory, *Chokepoints: Maritime Economic Concerns in Southeast Asia* (Washington: National Defense Univ. Press, 1996). For history: *Raffles of the Eastern Isles* by C.E. Wurtzburg (Hodder and Stoughton: London, 1954). There are two very interesting books about the garden: *Visions of Delight: The Singapore Botanic Gardens through the Ages* by Bonnie Tinsley, (Singapore Botanic Gardens: Singapore, 1989) and *A Pictorial Guide to The Singapore Botanic Gardens*, by Toy Eng Piu, Ohn Set, Christina Soh Jeng Har, Ali Ibrahaim and Ching Kok Ann (Singapore Botanic Gardens: Singapore, 1989). That intrepid Victorian, Marianne North has some interesting things to say also in *A Vision of Eden* (Webb & Bower Publishers Ltd.: Exeter, 1980.) Finally there is the fascinating story *The Marquis: A Tale of Syonan-to* by E.J. Corner (Heinemann Asia: Singapore, 1981).

The current Gardens director, Chin See Chung, responded to my questions with thoroughness and charm.

Henry Shaw's World Class Garden: The Missouri Botanical Garden

The Missouri Botanical Garden has published several very interesting documents. These include *Research at the Missouri Botanical Garden: The Unseen Garden* with text by Liz Forrestal Reinus (1993), as well annual reports which give a picture of not only the Garden's financial and educational activities during a year, but also of its research. The series of press releases on the Garden's publishing program, the individual gardens, and special events were both interesting and useful in getting a good fix on what is happening at the Garden. Two articles were particularly helpful, " One Hundred Years of the Missouri Botanical Garden" by Emanuel D. Rudolph, published in *Ann. Missouri Bot. Garden* 78: 1.18 1991 and "Henry Shaw's Idea of a Botanical Garden" published in the *Missouri Botanical Garden Bulletin*, Vol. XXXI, no. 7, p. 135, September 1943. And the booklet *Sculpture at the Missouri Botanical Garden* by George McCue (Missouri Botanical Garden: St. Louis, 1988) provided information about the sculptures which grace the Garden. Douglas Holland facilitated access to several archival photographs.

A long and interesting telephone conversation with the current director Dr. Peter Raven was extremely helpful, as were interviews with him published in several places. Of particular interest was the World Book Science Year interview, which is found at http://www.worldbook.com/fun/wbla/earth/html/ed04.htm. And as for evidence of human preferences for cues which suggests good savanna habitat, there are several studies of this including, "Cross-National Rankings of Tree Shape" *Ecological Psychology* 8 (4) 327 347, 1996 by Robert Sommer and Joshua Summit, and "Futher Studies of Tree Form Preference," *Ecological Psychology* 9 (2) 153-16 by Robert Sommer.

An American Kew...and Beyond: New York Botanical Garden

Much of the background history comes from *The New York Botanical Garden, An Illustrated Chronicle of Plants and People* by Ogden Tanner and Adele Auchincloss (Walker and Company: New York, 1991). Also useful were *A Walk through a World of Plants: The Enid A. Haupt Conservatory*, by Allen Appel (The New York Botanical Garden: New York, 1997) and *A Visit to the Garden: The New York Botanical Garden* (The New York Botanical Garden: New York, 2000.)

In writing this section, many publications of the NYBG were used. Among them were: Annual reports from 1997, 1998, and 1999, pamphlets about individual gardens within the garden and about the garden's forest, and longterm plans, 1993-1999 and 2001-2006. The article "Landscape for Learning," by Paul Bennett in *Landscape Architecture*, July 1998, gave much information about the Adventure Center. Karl Lauby was very helpful in seeing that I received the documents and photographs which I needed promptly.

A Garden to Educate and Delight a Nation: Montreal

Two sources consulted were particularly useful: *Étude historique et analyse patrimoiniale du Jardin botanique du Montréal* by Jacques Des Roches, commissioned by the Quebec Ministère de la culture et des communications, 1995, and *Le Jardin botanique de Montréal; esquisse d'une histoire* by André Bouchard, (Fides: Montréal, 1998). Also helpful was *Frederick Law Olmsted: Designing the American Landscape* by Charles E. Beveridge and Paul Rocheleau, (Rizzoli: New York, 1995) which is a beautiful book.

The director, Jean-Jacques Lincourt and former director Pierre Bourque, now mayor of Montreal, also provided much information. the aptly-named Normand Fleury provided archival photographs.

The Flowers of San Francisco

The director Scot Medbury, Collections Manager Bian Tan, and the staff at the Helen Crocker Russell Library were extremely helpful and generous with their time. Barbara Pitschel found several interesting archival photos. Among the many articles consulted were: a special issue of *California Horticultural Journal*, 1970, with articles by Russell Beatty and Elizabeth McClintock; a fact sheet prepared for Strybing docents, October 1992; "San Francisco's New Zealand Garden Legacy" by Scot Medbury in *Pacific Horticulture* January/ February/March 2000; and "Beyond Strybing: the Botanical Garden's Role in Plant Conservation" by Bian Tan in *Leaflet* Winter 2000.

In addition, I consulted: *California Patterns: A Geographical and Historical Atlas* by David Hornbeck (Mayfield Publishing Company: Palo Alto, CA, 1983) and *Frederick Law Olmsted: Designing the American Landscape* by Charles E. Beveridge and Paul Rocheleau (Rizzoli: New York, 1995).

University Garden on the Western Shore

Sources consulted include: "Botanical Garden of the University of British Columbia" by Gerald Straley, *Garden*, October, 1983; *The University of British Columbia Botanical Garden,* a publication of the University, by Josephine Bridge, 1995; *Guide to the Nitobe Memorial Garden* by Jo Bridge, Rachel Mackenzie, and Maurice M. Bridge, 1996; and "UBC Botanical Garden: Rich in History" by Patrica Parker, *Landmark,* March /April, 1993. In addition, Roy Taylor, David Tarrant, and Douglas Justice were very helpful. Dean Moura Quayle of the UBC Faculty of Agricultural Sciences shared her ideas with me. See also her article "The 21st Century Hybrid Landscape: Long and Winding Arboreta" in *Public Garden,* January/February/March 2000.

Passage to Juneau : A Sea and Its Meanings by Jonathan Raban, (Pantheon Books: New York, 1999) gives a detailed account of Raban's and Captain George Vancouver's voyages through the Strait of Georgia. The website of The Hunterian Museum at the University of Glasgow was also useful: http://www.hunterian.gla.ac.uk/HuntMus/cook/ Captain Cook: Voyages of Discovery.

Gardens of the Future

Two articles were useful: "Scientists and Religion in America" by Edward J. Larson and Larry Witham (*Scientific American,* September, 1999, p.88) and "Extinction Turns out to Be a Slow, Slow Process" by Andrew C. Revkin, (*New York Times,* D1, October 24, 2000).

Not to mention a marvelous website about gingkos which obviously is a labour of love by author Cor Kwant: http://www.xs4all.nl/~kwanten/history.htm.

Index

Véhicule Press

www.vehiculepress.com